T0265606

THE
FRAUD of TURIN

JAMES FRANCIS DAY

THE FRAUD OF TURIN
COPYRIGHT © 2023/2024 JAMES FRANCIS DAY

Published by:
Trine Day LLC
PO Box 577
Walterville, OR 97489
1-800-556-2012
www.TrineDay.com
TrineDay@icloud.com

Library of Congress Control Number: 2024939944

Day, James Francis.
–1st ed.
p. cm.

Epub (ISBN-13) 978-1-63424-476-3
Trade Paperback (ISBN-13) 978-1-63424-475-6
1. Christian art and symbolism. 2. RELIGION Christian Theology Christology.
3. Holy Shroud in art. 4. Holy Shroud History. 5. Church history. 6. Jesus Christ
Antiquities. I. Day, James Francis. Title

FIRST EDITION
10 9 8 7 6 5 4 3 2 1

Printed in the USA
Distribution to the Trade by:
Independent Publishers Group (IPG)
814 North Franklin Street
Chicago, Illinois 60610
312.337.0747
www.ipgbook.com

Publisher's Foreword

There's a sucker born every minute.
                                    – David Hannum

I'm a sucker for nice religious leaders. I fall for it every time.
                                    – Richard Dawkins

Religion was invented when the first con man met the first fool.
                                    – Mark Twain

Well, conmen are like that. A huckster is often a sucker for another huckster. I think they're people who get swept up in the moment. People who can convince themselves their crap is reality are very persuasive. They're also more likely to be swayed by the persuasiveness of another.
                                    – B.V. Larson

Having wondered often about the future, I'll ask myself: Why are we here? Is there a proper way to walk? Does it matter? The world's religions speak to these questions. According to Wikipedia:

> Religion is a range of social-cultural systems, including designated behaviors and practices, morals, beliefs, worldviews, texts, sanctified places, prophecies, ethics, or organizations, that generally relate humanity to supernatural, transcendental, and spiritual elements – although there is no scholarly consensus over what precisely constitutes a religion. Different religions may or may not contain various elements ranging from the divine, sacredness, faith, and a supernatural being or beings.

The Fraud of Turin delves into an object (icon) that has inflamed religious passions for over six centuries. First presented in 1354 in a church in the Champagne region of France, Lirey. The same area where the men who formed the Knights Templar hailed from. They had been "disbanded" by King Phillip IV of France on Friday, October 13, 1307 and on November 22, 1307 Pope Clement issued his papal bull *Pastoralis praeeminentiae* to arrest all Templars and seize their assets.

In 1312 Pope Clement officially abolished the Poor Fellow-Soldiers of Christ and of the Temple of Solomon, the formal name of the Knights Templar, and gave its remaining assets to The Order of Knights of the Hospital of Saint John of Jerusalem. Then in 1319 some of the Knights reformed in Portugal as the Order of the Knights of Our Lord Jesus Christ.

During these times there was much religious fervor: crusades, cathedral building and severe penitent displays. And much religious fraud: the selling of indulgences, selling of church offices and the selling of relics.

Author James Day unravels the murky history surrounding the "Shroud of Turin" and gives the reader rationales for the sudden appearance of the famed burial shroud. Then James diligently follows the Shroud, as it was "given" to the House of Savoy, and placed in a chapel in France, before being moved to Italy in 1578. Then to the Turin Cathedral in 1683 where it resides in the uniquely designed Chapel of the Holy Shroud to the present day.

This tachrichim (shroud) has had a long history of dispute. It was declared a forgery in 1389 by the Bishop of Troyes, and there is now a formal scholastic inquiry of the Shroud: sindonology, which looks into the veracity of the cloth and its history. It hasn't been shown publicly often. The Shroud was first photographed in 1898 and then in 1931. Both times the images created quite a stir with the negative of the image suggesting a positive image of the Holy Face of Jesus.

Interestingly, James began his work on this subject to try to authenticate the Shroud, but as he researched, he began to see the cracks in the established narrative. Rather than abandon the project he choose to follow the story where it led, and has produced a wonderful exposition of medieval and church history – *The Fraud of Turin*.

> *How easy it is to make people believe a lie, and [how] hard it is to undo that work again!*
>
> –Mark Twain

Onward to the Utmost of Futures!
Peace,
RA "Kris" Millegan
Publisher
TrineDay
July 16, 2024

We shall not cease from exploration, and the end of all our exploring will be to arrive where we started and know the place for the first time.
    – T.S. Eliot, *The Waste Land*

ACKNOWLEDGEMENTS

Many corresponded with me along the journey. Among them I thank Felix Ackermann; Fr. Michael Brunovsky, O.S.B.; Alessandro Camiz; Jannic Durand; Hugh Farey; Stephen Fliegel; Justin E.A. Kroesen; Mario Latendresse; Anne Lester; Nys Ludovic; J.P. Martin; Amanda Mikolic; Emmanuel Mouraire, Andrea Nicolotti; Guy Perry; Konstantinos T. Raptis; Laura Ricci; Donna L. Sadler; Christian Sapin; John Beldon Scott; Orit Shamir; Robert J. Spitzer, S.J.; Charlotte Stanford; Ian Wilson. And to the staff of the Garden Grove Main Library for the many Inter-Library Loan requests; to Kris Millegan and the TrineDay staff; and, as always, to Christina and the gals.

For My Parents

John William (1942-2011)
Mary Elizabeth (1948-)

Stat crux dum volvitur orbis
The Cross is steady while the world turns
Carthusian motto

Contents

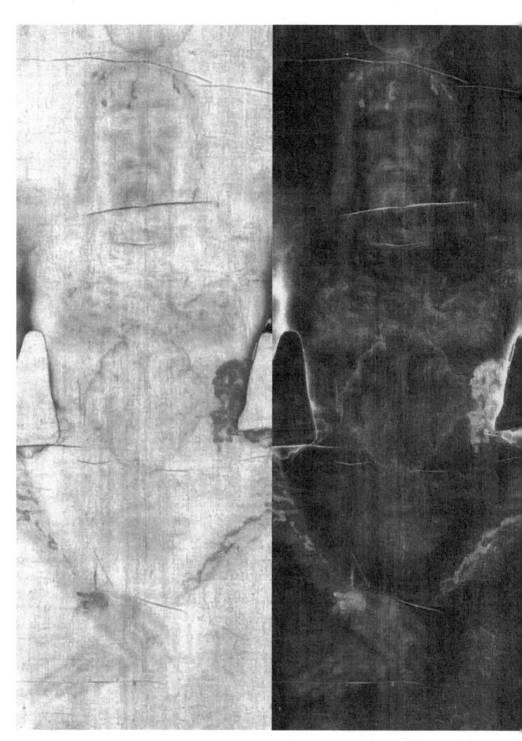

Frontal image on the Shroud of Turin, photograph by G. Enrie, 1931; positive and negative formats

PREFACE

There is a telling sequence in the epitaph of Conrad I, king of Upper Burgundy, who reigned until his death in AD 993, that summarizes the inherent worldview of the people we will meet in the pages ahead. The geography of this kingdom at this time, generally speaking, encompassed much of the landscape that concerns us. The part of the inscription reads, in its contemporary French translation: *Vous qui portez des vêtements précieux et qui accumulez sans fin des richesses qui ne vous profiteront pas, sachez que vous vous satisferez de peu de biens après votre trépas. Suffisent le linceul et la pierre;* that is, "You who wear precious clothes and who endlessly accumulate wealth that will not benefit you, know that you will be satisfied with few possessions after your death. *Sufficient the shroud and the stone.*"[1]

This work originally began as a manuscript detailing the various hypotheses on how the Shroud of Turin came into the possession of the Charny-Vergy families before coming into the possession of the House of Savoy in the mid-15th century. It also sought to summarize the various scientific studies carried out since the Carbon-14 Dating test of 1988 reported a medieval origin for the linen cloth (1260-1390).

In other words, I went into the project enchanted with the very real possibility the Shroud was not just a relic but evidence of the Resurrection of the Christ. This was the conclusion drawn by apologists of the Shroud in some Christian, especially Catholic, circles: even so far as the Shroud hoisted up as scientific proof of the Church's dogma that the crucified Jesus is in fact the Second Person of the Trinity, the Son of the everliving God.

What an incredible thing, then, this silent cloth, this silent witness to the most seismic event in the history of the world! Could this be what the Apostle John saw when he peered into the tomb as described in the Gospel of John, Chapter 20?

> 6. When Simon Peter arrived after him, he went into the tomb and saw the burial cloths there,
>
> 7. and the cloth that had covered his head, not with the burial cloths but rolled up in a separate place.

---

1   Robert Favreau, et al. *La ville de Vienne en Dauphiné* (Paris: CNRS Editions, 1990), 79-80. Emphasis mine.

Was the Shroud the item from the tomb, donated by Joseph of Arimathea, that survived centuries and a long stint in the Byzantine East? Was this the linen cloth witnessed by St. Peter?

Although I grew up in Catholic education in the years after the C-14 test of 1988 that effectively stripped the Shroud of any mysticism, a world called Shroud studies, or sindonology, believed the carbon dating was flawed, and that a number of intensive studies and tests by believers in the Shroud proved otherwise. The most stunning of these was a proposal from Italian physicist Paolo Di Lazzaro that the all-important image of the crucified Christ on the cloth was formed by pulses of immense ultraviolet light "having durations shorter than one forty-billionth of a second, and intensities on the order of several billion watts."[2]

The lifelike countenance as seen in photographic negatives of the image on the cloth apparently could not be replicated by any artist or in any lab. The only explanation was that the Shroud was a miracle … it really was that which the Gospels spoke of, a fine linen cloth that wrapped the body of the Lord following his crucifixion.

Needless to say, the implications of this cloth was seismic – spiritually, scientifically, and historically.

An all-consuming objective was put before me: get to the truth of the cloth no matter what.

And so my sojourn was akin to time traveling into the Christian past, into the kingdoms of Christendom, where legends and facts blended into the colorful epoch called the Middle Ages.

What soon became clear was a series of interrelated events and people from the same part of Europe where the Shroud first emerged in the historical record, the Champagne and Burgundy areas of modern-day France. It was also in Champagne and Burgundy where:

- the call to protect Jerusalem was first summoned by a French pope, Urban II;

- where the knights who formed the Order of the Templars were born;

- where St. Bernard of Clairvaux and his Cistercians quietly influenced Christendom with their spirituality and asceticism;

- where the glorious Gothic cathedrals first rose to awesome heights;

2   Quoted in Frank Viviano, "Why Shroud of Turin's Secrets Continues to Elude Science," *National Geographic*, April 17, 2015, https://www.nationalgeographic.com/history/article/150417-shroud-turin-relics-jesus-catholic-church-religion-science.

- where creative poets like Chretien de Troyes inspired courts and knights with stirring tales of King Arthur and the quest for the Holy Grail;

All of these incidents were unified by one specific thing, including the Shroud: devotion to Christ, namely, the Holy Sepulcher in Jerusalem.

As research progressed, the more I doubted the Shroud's authenticity: I could not reconcile the historical record with the contemporary attempts to explain how the image was formed onto the Shroud. I finally reached the point of no return when I studied the latest hypothesis currently accepted by sindonologists – the Particle Radiation Hypothesis. According to sindonologist Fr. Robert Spitzer, summarizing an explanation proffered by by biophysicist Jean-Baptiste Rinaudo and nuclear physicist Kity Little, a sudden atomic disintegration transpired wherein "the body would have become mechanically transparent allowing the frontal cloth to pass through the body and the dorsal part of the cloth to be drawn up through a created vacuum into the dorsal part of the body."[3] Hence the image on the Shroud – and an explanation for the younger carbon dating (1260-1390).

Hypothesis aside, the Carbon-14 dating corresponded with the first recorded appearance of the Shroud in Lirey, south of Troyes. The extant documentation from 1389-1390 involving Avignon pope Clement VII and legal documents into the 15th century contains ample documentation about the Shroud in Lirey and the clear attempts by the Lirey church canons to present the cloth as the actual burial cloth of Christ. As I discovered, this followed a playbook similar to other documented attempts to create a place of pilgrimage: see, for instance, the Shroud at Cadouin (which Clement VII also had to deal with, in 1394), another cloth claimed to be the burial shroud of Christ – two of over three dozen claims from the era regarding the burial sheet.

But more than that, I became almost existentially troubled as a lifelong Catholic. What gradually emerged to me turned out to be something entirely different than what I was digesting about the Shroud in all those books, videos, and lectures: pseudoscience and pseudohistory disguised as reality. And not just reality, but an almost obsessive push to make belief in the Shroud dogma. And if not dogma, then as rubber-stamped curriculum taught in Catholic studies and other apologetic coursework. It seemed irresponsible and not a little deceitful to peddle the Shroud as real, tangible, scientific *and*

---

3   Robert J. Spitzer, "The Image on the Shroud and Evidence of the Resurrection," *Ignatius Press,* March 2023.

miraculous proof in the Crucifixion *and* Resurrection – big business today – when there were enough red flags to question its veracity.

Moreover, it is entirely possible French knight Geoffroi de Charny (d. 1356), who built the Lirey church in which the Shroud was first kept, and who is generally recognized as the first known owner of the Shroud, knew nothing about it. He was constantly in motion, and Lirey was just one of several places which he lorded over. At the same time he is a recognized writer on the qualities of a knight, and correspondences with the bishop and pope from Charny are retained. Yet there is no mention of such an incredible relic ostensibly in his possession.

But if Charny knew nothing, then the church canons and the dean in particular, Robert de Caillac, not only knew about it, but likely commissioned it – the small Lirey church was their livelihood. Following Geoffroi's death protecting King Jean the Good against the English during the Hundred Years' War in 1356, and with his body all the way at Poitiers, might the Shroud have served as both a memorial for the fallen lord of Lirey while advertised for revenue purposes as the shroud of Christ, a *drap mortuaire*? The French landscape was devastated by war and the effects of plague; Geoffroi's widow ensured funds would be put in her infant son's name. Like other churches in this time, the Lirey church needed some kind of attraction to separate itself from others. That the canons put up such a fight over control of the Shroud with Marguerite, Geoffroi's granddaughter, until the bitter end (1453) suggests an ownership that leans towards the canons than it does the family Charny.

Corresponding with the primary source document from the Bishop of Troyes that the cloth was "cunningly painted," and taking into account the contemporary conclusions of University of Turin historian Andrea Nicolotti, the late chemical microscopist Walter McCrone, and photonics expert Joseph S. Accetta, my investigation leaned towards the Shroud as originating in the 14th century, with the image of the cloth created by a woodprint supplemented by paint.

But perhaps more than the cloth itself was the timeframe in which it appeared, given the proliferation of relics, their insatiable hold on the populace, and the desire for churches to attract pilgrims. Over this medieval milieu was a fascination, if not obsession, with the Passion of Christ. The Shroud of Turin fit precisely into this environment, where devotions surrounded the suffering Christ abounded: i.e. the Veil of Veronica, the icon of Man of Sorrows, Orthodox epitaphios, the feast of Corpus Christi

– literally the Body of Christ worshiped in the Eucharist of Holy Mass – itself a commemoration of the Crucifixion.

Unfortunately, there is little interest in placing the Shroud within this fascinating – and revealing – proper historical context. One might instead ask impatiently, *But what about the science?*

The problem is that the supposed science about the Shroud is promoted largely only by authenticists who are adamant in showing any possible way in which the Shroud can be from the time of Christ. For instance, the supposed Roman-era coin said to be visible on an eye is not championed by anyone outside the Shroud community. Dr. Max Frei's resume should make one suspect that he absolutely found the supposed pollens he claimed he collected from the Shroud. The post-Carbon 14 claims are also suspect. These are not indicative of the wider scientific community but are peddled by longtime Shroud supporters, i.e. Dr. John Jackson, Dr. Guilio Fanti and Dr. Di Lazzaro.

But what of the bloodstains? And the association with the sudarium of Oviedo? Three fragments of the sudarium of Oviedo were sent to C-14 labs between 1990 and 1992, each returning a dating between the sixth and ninth centuries. Another test was done in 2007 yielding the same results. The relationship between the Shroud and the sudarium is largely owed to sindonologist Fr. Giulio Ricci, whose book, *The Holy Shroud*, makes outrageous conclusions based on his study of the Shroud image.

The claim of blood, and specific blood type, is problematic. To date no reputable, accurate hematology tests have been conducted on the Shroud or the sudarium of Oviedo. The contradiction over the presence of blood on the Shroud versus no blood is too contradictory for a consensus to be reached. The claim of AB blood warrants serious reservation: someone who has type AB has no anti-A and anti-B antibodies. This means that blood which has no reaction is attributed to AB group. However, red ochre, which microscopist chemist Walter McCrone identified on the Shroud, when mistaken for blood will give a non-reaction, leading to the conclusion it must be AB.

The more I spent with the Shroud, then, the more it occurred to me that relying on it to propagate faith might be doing a disservice. Rather, exploring the rich milieu of history, tradition, creativity, and theology became of greater importance for me than validating the Lirey cloth now famous worldwide as the Shroud of Turin. I wanted both Christians and non-Christians to look upon this little-reported history of medieval creativity and perhaps help bridge our polarized world.

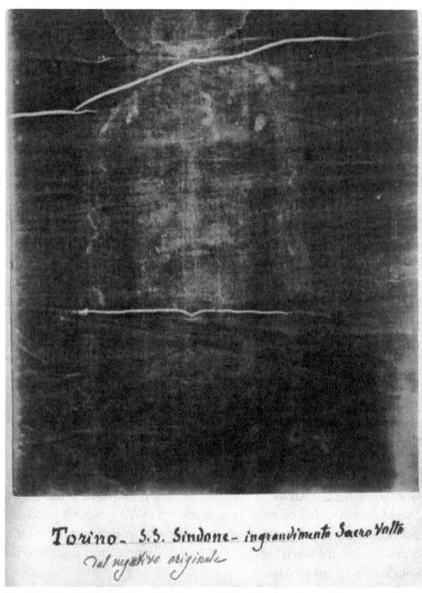

Torino - S.S. Sindone - ingrandimento Sacro Volto dal negativo originale

Secondo Pia's 1898 negative of the image on the Shroud of Turin has an appearance suggesting a positive image. It is used as part of the devotion to the Holy Face of Jesus. Image from Musée de l'Élysée, Lausanne.

Timeline: The Shroud's First Century (1353-1460)

T he following is a comprehensive timeline of documented events showing the controversy engulfing the presence of the Shroud, a controversy, ultimately, that amounts to nothing more than a provincial argument over a religious devotional object between canon regulars of a church and the family who founded it.

June 20, 1353: Geoffroi de Charny, a knight in service to the king of France, obtains from King Jean II an annual rent of 140 livres for foundation of church at Lirey, his fief just south of Troyes.

July 1353: Church at Lirey, Notre-Dame de Annunciation, is founded. Robert de Caillac is dean of the church, with a staff of six canons. The Act of Foundation makes no mention of a shroud.

January 30, 1354: Charny petitions for church at Lirey to be granted collegiate status by Pope Innocent VI, including an increase in indulgences and number of canons.

August 3, 1354: Pope Innocent VI grants indulgences.

Circa 1355: According to 1389 memorandum by Pierre d'Arcis, bishop of Troyes, sometime this year the Shroud is introduced in the Lirey church and displayed to pilgrims. It does not state how the cloth arrived in the church. At some point prior to his death in 1370, however, Troyes bishop Henri de Poitiers imposes a ban on showings claiming the "cloth" was "cunningly portrayed" in "a subtle manner" which attracted many people deceived by a false relic replete with false miracle stagings. To Bishop Henri, that an image was on the cloth flew in the face of the Gospels having never mentioned one. Also, following an investigation undertaken by Henri's orders, "it was even proved by the artist who had portrayed it that it was made by work of a man."

June 25, 1355: King Jean II bestows the port-oriflamme, the sacred banner of France, upon Geoffroi de Charny, the second time the knight received the honor.

May 28, 1356: During the octave of Corpus Christi, Troyes bishop, Henri de Poitiers, formally affirms the Lirey church as a collegiate church and praises

Charny on his faith and his success in establishing a "divine cult." The episcopal letter does not, however, mention the Shroud.

September 19, 1356: Defending King Jean II while bearing the oriflamme, Geoffroi de Charny dies at the battle of Poitiers.

November 1356: Charny's widow, Jeanne de Vergy, appeals to the dauphin, Charles V, to make grants formerly made out to her late husband to be changed to their son, Geoffroi II, still a minor.

1358-1359: Anglo-Navarrese troops terrorize and rampage the area around the Lirey church. The nearby Benedictine abbey of Montier-la-Celle is pillaged. According to Geoffroi II's 1389 statement, the Shroud is moved to a safe, hidden location during this English aggression phase of The Hundred Years' War.

1362: Now of age, Geoffroi II participates in his first military campaign, for the Count of Tancarville.

1370: Troyes bishop Henri de Poitiers dies. That same year, Charles V relocates Geoffroi de Charny's body from a Poitiers cemetery to the Abbey of the Celestines in Paris.

1373-1375: Further aggression by English cavalcades in the area around Lirey.

1377: Pierre d'Arcis is installed as bishop of Troyes.

April 8, 1378: Pope Urban VI is elected pope.

September 20, 1378: French cardinals, opposing election of Urban VI, elect Robert of Geneva who takes the name Clement VII, inciting the Avignon Papacy and thus the Western Schism. With the blessing from Charles V of France, the Catholic kingdoms of Castile, Aragon, Navarre, Joanna queen of Naples, Flanders, Scotland, Burgundy and Savoy support Clement.

Circa 1388: The Shroud returns to Notre-Dame de Lirey and is again exhibited.

Early 1389: Troyes bishop, Pierre d'Arcis, condemns the Shroud exhibitions at a synod in Troyes, specifically ordering all clergy in his diocese to not mention the Shroud whatsoever.

On or around April 6, 1389: Geoffroi II de Charny, in Sens, meets and appeals to Clement VII's papal legate, Pierre de Thury, for approval to have a place reserved in the Lirey church for the Shroud. Geoffroi II only vaguely mentions his father "had a place made with reverence for a certain figure or representation of our Lord Jesus Christ's shroud, offered him in generosity." The cardinal complies by issuing an indult, circumventing the episcopal authority of Pierre d'Arcis. The Shroud is installed in a place reserved for it in the church, and pilgrims again return to Lirey.

Mid-1389: D'Arcis orders the Lirey dean, Nichole Martin, under penalty of excommunication, to cease exhibitions. Martin refuses, and is summarily excommunicated by d'Arcis. Dean Martin appeals to Clement VII.

July 28, 1389: Pope Clement VII, in a letter to Geoffroi II, confirms Cardinal de Thury's indult, voiding d'Arcis's excommunication on dean Martin, specifically mentioning that those displaying the Shroud must notate it as a "figura seu representatio" of the Shroud of Christ, that is, as a "figure" or "image" or "(re) presentation."

Summer 1389: Geoffroi II appeals to King Charles VI for a royal safeguard, a kind of protection that would enable exhibitions to continue. In turn, an irate Pierre d'Arcis also appeals to Charles for intervention to stop the showings.

August 4, 1389: Siding with Bishop d'Arcis, parliament and king revoke the royal safeguard. Charles orders the bailiff of Troyes, Jean de Venderesse, to confiscate the Shroud and either relocate it to another Troyes church or elsewhere in custody of the king.

August 15, 1389: On the Feast of the Assumption, as canons prepare to showcase the Shroud, the procurator and sergeants of the king arrive at Lirey to claim the Shroud, bearing the king's letter. The dean claims it is not in his power to turn over the cloth. The procurator demands the church treasury to be opened. The dean claims he had only one key to the treasury and did not have access to the other keys. As it was nearing lunchtime, a seal was placed on the treasury door, effectively marking the treasury and its contents inside as property of the king, even though dean Martin claimed the Shroud was not actually in the treasury at that time. The sergeants then leave empty-handed.

September 5, 1389: Jean de Venderesse, bailiff, assigns his first sergeant, Jean de Beaune, to deliver letters to the canons at the Lirey church.

September 6, 1389: Jean de Beaune goes to Lirey and announces the Shroud is in property of the king of France. de Beaune also goes to the castle of Lirey to inform Geoffroi II, but Geoffroi is not home.

August 1389-January 1390: Pierre d'Arcis prepares a memorandum for Clement VII describing the events of the Shroud at Lirey and the deceitful manner in which it is shown, from the days when his predecessor, Henri de Poitiers, is believed to have uncovered the artist of the Shroud to the modern ostensions of it, as we have seen. His main gripe is that those at Lirey who exhibit the Shroud do so under false pretenses that the Shroud in fact is the true Shroud of Christ, thus amounting to idolatry.

January 6, 1390: A bull from Pope Clement VII rejects the position of d'Arcis and authorizes ostensions of the Shroud, again stating that clear signage or announcement must be delivered "stopping any deception," stating: "that the aforementioned figure or representation is not the true shroud of our Lord Jesus Christ, but a sort of depiction or painting made as a figure or representation of the shroud that is said to have been that of our Lord Jesus Christ himself."

May 30, 1390: A final version of the bull is sent to its recipients. Some verbiage is corrected, for instance, the phrase above now reads: "that the aforementioned figure or representation they display not as the true shroud of our Lord Jesus Christ, but as a figure or representation of the aforementioned shroud that is said to have been that of our Lord Jesus Christ himself." Clement also forbids clerics from exhibiting the Shroud in solemn liturgical dress so as to "remove any chance of error and idolatry."

June 1, 1390: Clement VII grants new indulgences for pilgrims: a year and forty days, not to pay homage or venerate the Shroud, but to visit the Lirey church. Such granting is common for churches dedicated to Our Lady.

1390: Geoffroi II embarks on the Barbary Crusade in service of Philippe II the Bold, Duke of Burgundy, who was fourteen and on the battlefield at Poitiers when Geoffroi de Charny died.

Around 1393: Marguerite de Charny, daughter of Geoffroi II and his wife, Marguerite de Poitiers, is born.

September 16, 1394: Pope Clement VII dies.

April 18, 1395: Bishop d'Arcis dies.

September 25, 1396: Geoffroi II participates in the defeat at Nicopolis, the battle that likely took his life.

Around 1412: Marguerite de Charny marries Jean de Bauffremont. The marriage produces no children.

October 25, 1415: Jean de Bauffremont dies in the Battle of Azincourt.

Around 1416: Marguerite de Charny marries Humbert de Villersexel. The marriage produces no children.

July 6, 1418: To avoid English aggression, the Shroud and other relics from Notre-Dame de Lirey are ushered to Humbert de Villersexel's estates in the Doubs Valley. A receipt with relics, including the Shroud, indicates the transfer. The Shroud is never returned to the canons of Notre-Dame de Lirey.

May 8 and 9, 1443: The Court of Dole rules the Shroud to be restituted to the Lirey canons. In this trial, Marguerite informs the court the Shroud was obtained in military combat by her grandfather, Geoffroi de Charny. Marguerite refuses to return the Shroud.

1446: Another trial is launched to recover the Shroud from Marguerite de Charny.

November 6, 1449: A proceeding with the Provost of Troyes from the Lirey canons to obtain the Shroud is held.

1452: Marguerite de Charny, who had been holding exhibitions of the Shroud in various cities, brings the Shroud to Chambery in Savoy territory.

On or around March 1453: Marguerite transfers the Shroud to her kinsmen, the Duke of Savoy, Louis I, and his wife, Anne of Cyprus. Interestingly, for a time Louis's father was an antipope, the ill-fated Felix V. It remains in the Savoy family until 1983 when the Shroud formally becomes property of the Holy See.

1457: The ecclesiastical court at Besancon excommunicates Marguerite de Charny for failing to comply to court orders in returning the Shroud.

July 7, 1460: Still under the pain of excommunication, Marguerite de Charny dies, and with her, the direct lineage of Geoffroi de Charny.

A poster advertising the 1898 exhibition of the shroud in Turin. Secondo Pia's photograph was taken a few weeks too late to be included in the poster. The image on the poster includes a painted face, not obtained from Pia's photograph.

"THE OTHER SIDE OF THE SHROUD"

by Jean de Joinville

It has recently come to my attention that my grandson, esteemed knight and counsellor to the king, Sir Geoffroi de Charny, is said to have come into possession of a linen cloth in which our Lord Jesus Christ was wrapped when His body lay in lonely repose on that slab of limestone in the tomb once owned by the Arimathean. Moreover, this same cloth is reported to bear a representation or likeness, a sort of shadowy outline depicting how our Lord appeared within the cloth – indeed, some are claiming, impressed on the cloth by unexplainable scientific methods only the Angelic Doctor would understand – at the very moment of our Lord's Resurrection!

The scenario has left me not a little perplexed.

I admire my grandson's military accomplishments (even if he found himself imprisoned on more than one occasion), but why would ecclesiastical authorities permit such a hallowed first-class relic, a Passion relic no less, to be exhibited out of the blue in my grandson's tiny hamlet church in rather obscure Lirey (property which I once owned), within the Diocese of Troyes, in Champagne? You see, my grandson Geoffroi is a busy man. He is constantly traveling to and fro across the kingdom and even into lands under interdict. By this I mean, he has never provided documentation stating from whence the linen came. In fact, he has never uttered a word about it. Perplexing, indeed.

As retired seneschal of Champagne, and with plenty of time on my hands [having died in 1317] , I therefore set out to conduct my own investigation on the nature of this Mysterious Cloth. I have concluded this investigation after all these years, nay centuries, and here catalog some claims about this shroud's provenance and counter-claims I have amassed.

I. On the claims that the Shroud is "The Image of Edessa," or, The Mandylion...

Aside from the lack of detail about the Shroud's origins whether in Lirey or in the Gospels, a problem we noticed straightaway was the Edessa icon had no connection with that of the *burial cloth* of our Lord, let alone His Passion. Rather, the story goes, King Abgar of Osroene became privy to the tales of miracles performed by Christ Jesus by an aide who witnessed them first hand, Ananias. Ananias then returned to Judea with a letter from Abgar and began to draw a portrait of Jesus. After replying to Abgar with His own letter, Jesus washed His face and dried it on a towel, the result of which – "in some divine and inexpressible manner"[1] – was an impression of His holy face. Jesus promised the relic would offer much protection and grace for the people of Edessa. Not only did the cloth cure Abgar upon the king laying eyes on the imprinted face of Jesus, but Abgar was soon baptized, his action converting the whole of Edessa to Christianity. And thus a miraculous image of Christ was responsible for the conversion of an Arab country.

It seems that only in the twentieth century was the image of Edessa hypothesized to be the Shroud of Turin folded four times, like a towel, and encased within a protective tile for hundreds of years.[2] Thus, no one really knew the hidden icon was in fact the most holy shroud of Christ. *This is only an assumption*, and should be acknowledged as such when discussing the origins of this shroud.

Now what of the numerous similar iconographic elements of icons of Christ and the likeness on the Shroud, indeed claims that the Shroud is the prototype of every artistic depiction of Christ?

Paul Vignon, stalwart supporter of the Shroud in the early twentieth century, is normally attributed for the "Vignon Markings," a number of features he identifies on the Shroud as congruent with traits common to depictions of Christ in Byzantine art, such as the frontal arch, from eyebrows to stem of nose, swollen cheek, and forked beard. Therefore, so went Vignon's conclusion, that the Shroud, with the authentic image of Christ, served as the prototype for all subsequent depictions of Him, including those of the dead Christ on *epitaphioi*, Orthodox liturgical cloths. For Vignon, who did not equate the Shroud as the image of Edessa, even the painter of the Edessa image actually referenced the Shroud in creating the image of the Holy Face.

This idea has been advanced by I. Wilson and Heinrich Pfeiffer, SJ, among others. Gian Marco Rinaldi termed the practice the "theory of iconographic sindonocentrism." It's a foolproof approach to say everything derived from the Shroud, from thirteenth century entombment scenes that populated eastern France to all the mosaics of Christ in both the east and

---

1 Herbert L. Kessler, *Spiritual Seeing: Picturing God's Invisibility in Medieval Art* (Philadelphia: University of Pennsylvania Press, 2000), 70-71.

2 Ian Wilson, *Holy Faces, Secret Places: An Amazing Quest for the Face of Jesus* (New York: Doubleday, 1991), 130-144, sp. 142.

west that followed the basic facial patterns. In this way, despite any substantive proof or backing by any art historians of repute, those who desire can claim the Shroud's authenticity following this line of argument.

II. On the claims of the Shroud's journey from Edessa to Constantinople (944-1204)...

The transfer of the facecloth icon of Christ from Moslem-controlled Edessa to Constantinople in August 944 was overseen by General John Kourkas in exchange for two hundred Muslim prisoners. The event is commemorated as a minor feast on the Byzantine calendar, the Translation of the Icon Not Made by Human Hands. Archdeacon Gregory Referandarius, in his homily for the liturgy celebrating the mandylion's arrival, cited it as the cloth Christ wiped His face with in the Garden of Gethsemane "when his sweat became like drops of blood."[3]

When the Shroud was finally displayed in Lirey, according to this proposal, the mandylion/Shroud was at last exposed in full. However, historians such as Steven Runciman and Averil Cameron identify the mandylion as part of the passion reliquary purchased by my own friend Louis IX from his cousin, Baldwin II, last Latin emperor of Constantinople in 1247. It is sure that the icon was destroyed, like most of France's Catholic culture, in the French Revolution.

On its face, though, the idea of the Shroud as the mandylion initially seems reasonable. But the story of this image of Edessa is one where Jesus is still alive; the Shroud, of course, emphasizes the dead Christ. The very definition of the mandylion evokes a small napkin or handkerchief – the Holy Face – while the Shroud's identity is synonymous with the full body. But even this conflict has a response, in the account of Picardy knight Robert de Clari, whose on-the-ground chronicle of the Fourth Crusade includes a ritual in St. Mary of Blachernae wherein:

> And among those other there was another church which was called My Lady Saint Mary of Blachernae, where there was the shroud (sydoines) in which Our Lord had been wrapped, which every Friday raised itself upright so that one could see the form of Our Lord on it, and no one, either Greek or French, ever knew what became of this shroud (sydoines) when the city was taken.[4]

---

3   Lk 22:44. For analysis on Referandarius, Gerhard Wolf, "From Mandylion to Veronica" in *The Holy Face: Paradox of Representation*, ed. Wolff and Herbert Kessler (Electa: Italy, 1999). See also Andrea Nicolotti, *From the Mandylion of Edessa to the Shroud of Turin* (Leiden: Brill Academic, 2014).
4   Robert de Clari, *The Conquest of Constantinople*, trans. Peter Dembowski (Paris: Champion, 1904), 90.

This is often seized as evidence that such an object was the Shroud of Turin. It is important to note, however, Clari is only reporting what he has heard, not seen.[5] Additionally, as Jean-Pierre Martin observed, "no evidence that this lost *sydoines* which Robert de Clari would therefore have never have been able to see, is actually the same relic as the Shroud."[6]

Even if Clari's shroud was a burial cloth, it was one of many from Constantinople. Nineteenth century researcher Count Riant's sprawling and detailed documentation of the dispersion of relics even names one Robert de Clari as bringing a fragment of Christ's burial shroud back home to Picardy, to Corbie abbey.[7] Once again, a "smoking gun" reference to the unique characteristics of the Shroud of Turin is nowhere to be found in the catalog of relics shipped from Byzantium to the Latin West in the wake of the ignoble Fourth Crusade.

III. On the claims of the Shroud's journey from mighty Constantinople to my grandson's hamlet of Lirey (1204-c. 1355)...

When western crusaders sacked Constantinople in 1204, the story goes, the cloth of Christ disappeared, removed from the imperial church's Pharos Treasury and ushered out of the city.[8] The usual culprit is identified as wily Burgundian knight Othon de la Roche, who founded the duchy of Athens and became its first lord. No chronicler of the crusade, such as Geoffroi de Villehardouin, mentions such a prized passion relic in de la Roche's possession. The de la Roche angle was hatched from a purported letter written to Pope Innocent III from one Theodore Angelos, brother of Michael, Despot of Epirus. Theodore Angelos's letter, dated August 1, 1205, complains to the pope about the Latin treatment of Constantinople's wealth of sacred relics:

> The Venetians partitioned the treasures of gold, silver, and ivory while the French did the same with the relics of the saints and the most sacred of all, the linen in which our Lord Jesus Christ was wrapped after his death and before the resurrection. We know that the sacred objects are preserved by their predators in Venice, in France, and in other places, the sacred linen in Athens.[9]

---

5 Andrea Nicolotti, *The Shroud of Turin: The History and Legends of the World's Most Famous Relic*, trans. Jeffrey M. Hunt and R.A. Smith (Waco: Baylor UP, 2019), 45, citing Dobschütz, *Christusbilder* (Leipzig: Hinrichs, 1899), 77.

6 J.P. Martin, "Notes sur le manuscrit de Bruxelles de Garin le Lorrain," in *Convergences medievales*, ed. N. Henrard et al. Brussels: De Boeck and Larcier (2001), 325-326.

7 Paul Riant, *Exuviae sacrae Constantinopolitanae*, II (Paris: Ernest Leroux, 1904), 176.

8 For instance, Gerard Barbet, *Othon de La Roche: chroniques sur l'étonnante histoire d'un chevalier comtois devenu seigneur d'Athènes* (Besançon: Fortis, 2012).

9 Noel Currer-Briggs, *The Shroud and the Grail: A Modern Quest for the True Grail* (London: Weiden-

The letter as an authentic document is in serious question, with only a supposed Latin translation from the 19th century the extant document.[10] While there is ample documentation of correspondence between Pope Innocent and Othon de la Roche in the official files of Innocent III, as well as with Innocent's successor, Honorius III, there is neither a mention of a shroud nor Theodore Angelos' complaint about one.[11] Often in Shroud presentations audiences are told Othon passed the Shroud off to his father, Pons de la Roche, who then dutifully donated it to the local cathedral of Besançon, St. Etienne. About 150 years later, a convenient fire in the cathedral resulted in the Shroud's rescue, which subsequently ended up in the possession of my Geoffroi de Charny. Professor Andrea Nicolotti of the University of Turin, however, unmasks the origins of this storyline as an invention from the eighteenth century by Pierre-Joseph Dunod. In fact, Nicolotti devoted a whole book on the shroud of Besançon, published in 2015 (*Le Saint Suaire de Besançon et le chevalier Othon de La Roche*).

Another strand supporters of the de la Roche angle like to follow is that Othon de la Roche is an ancestor of my grandson's second wife, Jeanne de Vergy. The conclusion, then, is that the Shroud somehow passed down from Othon to Othon II to his daughter, who married Henry I de Vergy to Jean I de Vergy to Guillaume de Vergy and finally to Jeanne de Vergy. Yet we have no record of Jeanne de Vergy owning the Shroud, either as a dowry or in a will. If this were the case, there likely would not have been the legal drama that plagued Jeanne and Geoffroi's granddaughter, Marguerite de Charny, the last Charny holder of the Shroud, against the canons of the Lirey church over rightful possession of this odd cloth. Such a sad state of affairs ended with Marguerite excommunicated from Holy Mother Church for her antics regarding the Shroud. She died in 1460.

In all the documentation extant on the Lirey cloth, no one has ever talked about a dual-sided cloth bearing the faint image of Christ until it actually publicly appeared to much controversy and fanfare, albeit if only locally.

---

feld and Nicolson), 147. The rest of the hypothesis usually follows the narrative that Othon de la Roche handed off the Shroud to his father, Pons de la Roche (others say it was kept in the Castle of Ray in Haute-Saone), who in turn handed it off to the St. Etienne cathedral in Besançon. After a fire in 1349, the Shroud was rescued and somehow got to Geoffroi de Charny.

10 See Andrea Nicolotti, "Su alcune testimonianze del Chartularium Culisanense, sulle false origini dell'Ordine Costantiniano Angelico di Santa Sofia e su taluni suoi documenti conservati presso l'Archivio di Stato di Napoli" in Giornale di storia 8 (2012).

11 See Innocent III, *Opera Omnia, I-IV* (PL, 214-217) 215 col. 1270sq; 345f (sermon).

Here I would like to add a bit of disappointment that when considering the Shroud's background, only shrewd de la Roche is considered. There are any number of noblemen who might have passed the Shroud down. What of my ancestors? My uncle, Geoffroi V, took the cross for both Richard the Lionheart's crusade (the Third Crusade) and returned for the Fourth Crusade, indeed dying in Syria, at the Krak des Chevaliers. His brother, Andre, was a Templar. Another brother, Robert, teamed up under Gauthier of Brienne's army but died in Apulia. Not only was Geoffroi V tethered to Clairvaux abbey and the Cistercians, as was I, but he was associated with Geoffroi Villehardouin and Simon de Montfort.

And still more: what of those Briennes? Walter VI Brienne was a fellow member of the Order of the Star with my grandson, Geoffroi. Both served the king, indeed dying for him at Poitiers. Did he know about the Shroud? James I, Count de la Marche, was also at Poitiers. He was the maternal great-grandfather of Anne of Cyprus, wife of Duke Louis of Savoy, who took possession of the Shroud from Marguerite. Did de la Marche know about the Shroud?

Did the king? If it was Philippe VI the Valois who gave Geoffroi the Shroud for a job well done, why did his later successor Louis XI attempt to intervene and claim it? Still yet, would not Louis IX just as well gifted me the Shroud for a job well done?

All good questions, I should say.

About the Author
Jean de Joinville (c. 1224-1317) is the lord of Joinville, seneschal of Champagne, Seventh Crusade veteran, and chronicler of the hagiographic *Histoire de St Louis, Roi de France*. He lives in his castle at Joinville, France with his nine children and three cocker spaniels: Dusty, Pickles, and Sherwood Williams. He can be reached by pigeon carrier.

Cimabue's Crucifixion in the Upper Basilica of Saint Francis of Assisi (late 13th c.) in positive and negative photographic elements. The fresco colors have deteriorated over time, resulting in de facto photographic negatives. Paul Vignon dismissed any such similarities to the Turin Shroud

PART I
THE LOST WORLD
OF CHRISTENDOM

The Seige of Acre. William of Clermont defends Ptolemais, 1291, by Dominique-Louis Papety, 1845.

CHAPTER ONE

THE COLLAPSE OF A DREAM

In Mary 1291 with the fall of Acre, then the Latin Holy Land strong-hold after the surrender of Jerusalem a century earlier, the Latin West's dreams of reclaiming Jerusalem and restoring it to the extent it had reached in the twelfth century practically vanished. The Jerusalem High Court fled to Cyprus where a western presence remained for another two hundred years and Cyprus in fact flourished, despite the overall failure to regain Jerusalem proper.

After all, the initial crusade of 1095-1099, as preached by the Champagne-born, Benedictine monk Pope Urban II, was about not only possession of a land as much as it was seizing an ideal, to wrestle *ubilu-cum mundi*, the center of the world, from the infidel and to return its hallowed place where Christ died, descended into hell, and rose again. "There remained the ultimate relic," Robert Payne wrote of Urban II, "the empty tomb in the Church of the Holy Sepulcher. Indeed, for him the Holy Land was itself a relic, a place of surpassing holiness, and he was determined to conquer it."[1]

Born into the noble house of Lagery around 1035, the future fifth pope from France was raised in the Diocese of Chalons-Sur-Marne, near the battlefield where Attila the Hun was turned away from his Gal-lic advance six centuries earlier. At the time young Otho was preparing for a clerical life this area was ruled independent of the king of France by the count of Champagne. However, it was the local cathedral in Reims, named Notre-Dame, that held the coronation ceremony of every new monarch of France; a tradition that occurred, nearly unbroken, until the final coronation of a French monarch, that of Charles X, in 1825. The reason for the Reims cathedral in northeastern France as the location of coronation dates back to King Clovis – it was here where he was bap-tized by Saint Remigius on Christmas Day in 496. The anointing of the king during the coronation ceremony was a direct evocation of Clovis's anointing at baptism.

---

1 Robert Payne, *The Dream and the Tomb* (New York: Cooper Square Press, 2000), 336.

Five versions of the call for a crusade by Urban II, delivered at the Council of Clermont on November 27, 1095, have come down to us, as here from the account of Guibert de Nogent:

> If in olden times the Maccabees attained to the highest praise of piety because they fought for the ceremonies and the Temple, it is also justly granted you, Christian soldiers, to defend their liberty of your country by armed endeavor. If you, likewise, consider that the abode of the holy apostles and any other saints should be striven for with such effort, why do you refuse to rescue the Cross, the Blood, the Tomb?

In the second book of Maccabees, alluded by Urban, the prophet Jeremiah brazenly takes it upon himself to protect the Holy of Holies:

> When Jeremiah arrived there, he found a chamber in a cave in which he put the tent, the ark, and the altar of incense; then he sealed the entrance. Some of those who followed him came up intending to mark the path, but they could not find it. When Jeremiah heard of this, he reproved them: "The place is to remain unknown until God gathers his people together again and shows them mercy. Then the Lord will disclose these things, and the glory of the Lord and the cloud will be seen, just as they appeared in the time of Moses and of Solomon when he prayed that the place might be greatly sanctified."[2]

The prophet Jeremiah is thought to have been present in the Levant from about 626 BC to the siege of Jerusalem by Babylonian king Nebuchadnezzar II, the subsequent fall of the city, and destruction of Solomon's Temple in 587 BC. It was the Book of Jeremiah that contained the last reference of the Ark of Covenant, among 200 throughout the Old Testament until here in Second Maccabees. Following the reign of King Solomon, references to the Ark vanish. Jeremiah himself warned that in the end times:

> When you increase in number and are fruitful in the land – oracle of the LORD—They will in those days no longer say, "The ark of the covenant of the LORD!"
> They will no longer think of it, or remember it, or miss it, or make another one.[3]

It was Jeremiah, the relentlessly tortured prophet, who speaks of God's promise to establish a new covenant with the house of Israel, a theme that

---

2   2 Maccabees 2:5-8
3   Jeremiah 3:16

would speak directly to future crusading armies into Jerusalem: "They will be my people, and I will be their God."[4]

The evocation of the Maccabee as protector and defender of the holiest tabernacle stirred Frankish knights into dreaming likewise. Another version of Urban's address, by Robert the Monk, has Urban correlating the legacy of Charlemagne with the Tomb of the Holy Sepulchre, which was destroyed by the Fatimid Caliph Al-Hakim in 1009 and restored by Byzantine emperor Constantine IX Monomachos three decades later:

> Let the deeds of your ancestors move you and incite your minds to manly achievements; the glory and greatness of king Charles the Great, and of his son Louis, and of your other kings, who have destroyed the kingdoms of the pagans, and have extended in these lands the territory of the holy church. Let the holy sepulcher of the Lord our Savior, which is possessed by unclean nations, especially incite you, and the holy places which are now treated with ignominy and irreverently polluted with their filthiness. Oh, most valiant soldiers and descendants of invincible ancestors, be not degenerate, but recall the valor of your progenitors.

The count of Champagne at the time of Urban II's summons for a crusade, a young man named Hugh, later cultivated a strong friendship with an influential Cistercian monk in the region, Saint Bernard of Clairvaux (1090-1153). In a radical life decision, Hugh ultimately abandoned his own prestigious title, handed over his land to the Cistercians and relocated to Jerusalem, where he was among the first knights of a new monastic order with a decidedly military bent, a novel fusion of knighthood and monasticism, the Poor Fellow Soldiers of Christ and of the Temple of Solomon – an order better known as the Knights Templar. A vassal to this former count-turned-knight morphed into the order's First Grand Master, Hugues de Payens.

In another account of Urban's November 27 speech, Fulcher of Chartres documented Urban's summation to assist the Latin church's estranged Greek brethren. Constantinople at this time evoked less of her exotic beauty of the past than a decaying Rome when barbarians were at the Eternal City's gates. In this case, Seljuk Turks occupied most of Anatolia (the majority of modern-day Turkey) after defeating the Byzantines at the Battle of Manzikert in 1071. Now, as the Turks loomed over Constantinople, Byzantine Emperor Alexios I Komnenos was prompted to seek Latin aid whether he liked it or not.

---

4 Jeremiah 32:38

That Alexios reached out to the West indicates the seriousness of the dilemma. Urban II's predecessor, Pope Gregory VII, excommunicated Alexios – this was only decades after the Schism of 1054 – but Urban II lifted it upon his ascension to the papacy in 1088 in his shrewd attempt to keep communication open. Additionally, the Byzantines were weighed down in an ongoing series of struggles with numerous forces, like the ongoing Arab-Byzantine Wars, dating back to the time of Mohammed himself. After Muslim expansion surged into former Byzantine-held strongholds of Syria, Egypt, and Carthage in North Africa, numerous caliphates sought to claim the greatest prize, the heart of the empire, Constantinople. A later resurgence in Byzantine strength saw the eastern empire regain ground into the Adriatic Sea and eastern Italy, particularly Bari, while Sicily remained under the Muslim Moors. A unique Byzantine-Arab hybrid culture spawned in Sicily at this time. It ended with the Norman invasion of Sicily and with Norman rule after the successful siege of Palermo in 1091, became the Kingdom of Sicily.

Yet Constantinople soon had to contend with a new enemy when the Seljuk Turks rode down from the steppes of Central Asia, defeating the Byzantines at the Battle of Manzikert in 1071, claiming Anatolia and sweeping away caliphates all the way to Jerusalem. The Turks also attempted their own unsuccessful siege of Constantinople. Norman mercenaries were again engaged in battle, hired by the Byzantines to repel the Turks. Though they were deprived of Constantinople the Turks still threatened, and Alexios I was nervous – so nervous he wrote to the pope.

> For your brethren who live in the east are in urgent need of your help, and you must hasten to give them the aid which has often been promised them. For, as the most of you have heard, the Turks and Arabs have attacked them and have conquered the territory of Romania as far west as the shore of the Mediterranean and the Hellespont, which is called the Arm of St. George. They have occupied more and more of the lands of those Christians, and have overcome them in seven battles. They have killed and captured many, and have destroyed the churches and devastated the empire. If you permit them to continue thus for awhile with impurity, the faithful of God will be much more widely attacked by them.

Urban's reference to the "Arm of St. George" was a nickname for the Bosphorus strait coined by frequent Latin travelers. St. George was widely admired by both the Greek and Latin Christians, particularly by the knightly class who found inspiration in George's military derring-do. Not only was St. George an historical figure, an eastern Christian said to have been martyred by decapitation in Nicomedia in northern Anatolia (Turkey) during the persecutions of Diocletian in 303 AD, he was also a patron saint for the Christians of the First Crusade. Indeed, upon returning to his homeland following the conquest of Jerusalem and the establishment of the Latin kingdom in the Levant, Robert II, Count of Flanders was given the sacred relic of St. George's arm by Alexios I. The two formed such a relationship over the crusade that Alexios asked the count to remain in Constantinople as an adviser to the emperor and attaché on Byzantine diplomatic missions. When Robert declined, preferring instead to return to Flanders, Alexios presented him the relic. Robert then had the relic installed in the Benedictine Anchin Abbey in Flanders, whose abbot, Haymeric, was a close acquaintance of Urban II and present at the Council of Clermont.

Finally, Urban sealed his passionate speech with the most tempting of promises to his Catholic sons and daughters: "All who die by the way, whether by land or by sea, or in battle against the pagans, shall have immediate remission of sins."

What prompted Pope Urban II to boldly call for such a massive campaign for a land three thousand miles away that would take years to actualize, and possibly not even succeed? It was certainly not an impetuous decision. Prior to the Council of Clermont in November 1095, Urban spent weeks trotting with his prestigious entourage throughout France, offering an extremely rare encounter for local peasants and lords alike to glimpse the Supreme Pontiff. Meanwhile, Urban gauged the populace; could he rally enough religious fervor among the masses? The visibility would later pay off in the rousing speech on November 27.

Whether or not the letter from Alexios to Urban is genuine, it was unavoidable to notice the crescent moon of Islam was rising over the map of the known world. The very existence of Christendom was at stake. What better way to turn European counts, barons, and knights into a unified force and make the threat into a quest of recovering what was most holy to soldiers of Christ.

The crusader route was long and arduous, a journey that took nearly four years since the call for the crusade. Pope Urban II died on July 29, 1099 at Rome, only two weeks after Latin Christians successfully completed the final stage of the aggressive and bloody siege of Jerusalem when governor Iftikhar al-Dawla surrendered the city to Raymond IV, Count of Toulouse. Yet it was a surrender that did not transpire without a fight.

The crusader armies, having arrived at the Jerusalem walls from the road to Jaffa without issue, had split up for the siege, pitching camps at various parts of the city walls. al-Dawla expelled all Christian inhabitants of Jerusalem leading up to the inevitable battle with the crusaders. The Muslims within Jerusalem of whom al-Dawla governed were not the Seljuk Turks the crusaders encountered in Anatolia but Shia members of the Fatimid Caliphate from Egypt. al-Dawla had himself only assumed governorship of Jerusalem that very year, 1099, when the Fatimids defeated the Seljuks for control of Palestine. This change of hands is just one example of the rotating rulers of Middle East territory at the time, displaying the tenuous control any one group had on the Holy Land. To Christians, this was tangible enough evidence of its perilous state. It had been almost four hundred years since the occupation of the Umayyad Caliphate in Jerusalem, when the Dome of the Rock and the al-Aqsa Mosque were constructed in the eighth century.

After the first attempt to scale the city walls failed, the crusaders devised not a military strategy but a spiritual one – a barefoot procession of prayer and supplication replete with hymnal chanting around the 2½ mile wall in an act of penance and fasting. Aided by eleventh hour supplies from Genoese ships, which arrived at Jaffa, and privy to a collating Fatimid army from Egypt preparing to advance, despairing crusade forces scrambled to mount another assault on July 14. Godfrey of Bouillon and his troops were the first to scale the wall, near the Damascus Gate (dubbed St. Stephen's Gate by the crusaders for its proximity to the site of the first Christian martyrdom). The next day, victory in reach, crusaders rampaged through the city in a violent, ruthless final assault.

On July 22, with Christian holy sites secured by the crusaders, at a council meeting in the Church of the Holy Sepulchre, Godfrey of Bouillon was offered king of the newly minted Latin Kingdom of Jerusalem. Godfrey accepted but declined the title, instead choosing to call himself *Advocatus Sancti Sepulchri*, Advocate of the Holy Sepulchre. In choosing this name, Godfrey is to have solemnly declared there is only one true king of Jerusalem, the King of Kings, Jesus Christ.

No sooner was Jerusalem secured when its new occupants were forced to again engage in battle, at Ascalon, the final conflict consisting of all the major figures of the First Crusade. Located along the coast south of the city, the crusaders chose to advance towards Ascalon rather than wait for the 20,000-strong Fatimid army of al-Afdal, a vizier of the Fatimid caliphs of Egypt, to encroach Jerusalem. The crusading army was led into the struggle by the first Latin Patriarch of Jerusalem, Arnulf of Charques, as he carried the True Cross. The Battle of Ascalon proved victorious for the crusaders, led by Godfrey of Bouillon, but they did not completely banish the Fatimid army from the land until the Second Battle of Ascalon almost sixty years later, in 1153.

Following Godfrey's victory at Ascalon, the work of cultivating a new kingdom could begin, one safe for western pilgrims to journey and pray

The Holy Sepulcher, Jerusalem, 1910

at the now liberated holiest sites of Christendom. These included the Upper Room, where Jesus and his apostles celebrated the Last Supper; the Garden of Gethsemane, where Jesus was betrayed by Judas Iscariot and arrested; and the *Via Dolorosa*, the Way of the Cross. Yet by far the most important site to the Latin conquerors was that of the Church of the Holy Sepulcher, which enclosed both the empty tomb of Christ and the site of Jesus's crucifixion at Calvary. Originally outside the walls of the city in Christ's time, these locations were enveloped within Jerusalem proper when King Herod Agrippa I ordered construction of Jerusalem's Third Wall.

In the main, homesick and exhausted infantrymen who toiled behind the knights and nobles longed for their lands and families back home, eager to tell of all they accomplished and saw: of the glorious and mysterious Constantinople; of exotic Saracens and Muslims; of the Egyptians rearing to attack; of the immense spoils of war; of the unbelievable cities of the near Orient such as the mesmerizing Antioch with its staggering fortifications; and, not least of all, the experience of being in Jerusalem, of climbing its walls and entering its empty tomb within the Church of the Holy Sepulchre. To these crusaders fulfilling what Urban II promised years earlier, Jerusalem truly was the Heavenly City on earth. Most of these men, however, while perhaps spiritually cleansed from the expedition, returned with little more than stories and scars.[5]

Upkeep of the kingdom of Jerusalem, dubbed *Outremer* by the crusaders ("the land beyond the sea"), was an enormous undertaking. Constantly replenishing troops, pacifying subjects of distant territories, and continually needing to fortify Jerusalem itself gradually weakened the Latin grip on the Holy Land. In the 1140s, two pivotal figures died within a year of each other, Fulk of Anjou, king of Jerusalem, and Byzantine emperor John II Komnenos, leaving much of Outremer without any real significant leader. Imad ad-Din Zengi took advantage of the void and captured Edessa on Christmas Eve, 1144. Obsessed with taking Damascus, Zengi was eventually assassinated by a Frankish slave in 1146, and succeeded by his son, Nur ad-Din. During this heightened time of Muslim aggression against the Latin states in Palestine, a young Sunni boy was growing up in Mosul under the protection of Zengi and Nur ad-Din, *atabeg* (governor) of Aleppo and Mosul. His name was Saladin.

The Second Crusade was organized as a response to this aggressive expansion, its chief advocate Christendom's most respected voice, Bernard

---

5 Christopher Tyerman, *God's War: A New History of the Crusades* (London: Penguin UK, 2007), 175.

of Clairvaux. By now Bernard was the grey eminence behind the papal throne, especially with the current pope, Eugene III (d. 1153). After all, Eugene III was a Cistercian, the first of the order to become pontiff, and was a monk from Bernard's Clairvaux monastery before his elevation to the college of cardinals. Led by King Louis VII and his then-wife, Eleanor of Aquitaine, the Second Crusade failed to retake Edessa or fortify the kingdom in general. Steadily, the Latin kingdom was losing more territory, namely to Saladin, an antagonist for Christians who King Richard the Lionheart and King Philip Augustus could not tame in the Third Crusade. It was Saladin, sultan of Egypt and Damascus, who took Jerusalem in October 1187, forcing the capital of the kingdom north to the port city of Acre. A century later, however, even Acre fell.

The defeat at Acre in 1291 was the fatal blow to Latin control of the Holy Land. Yet even the squeezing of the formerly expansive Kingdom of Jerusalem onto the island of Cyprus did not mean there was no lack of calls to mount another crusade. An adviser to King Philip IV, Pierre Dubois, was so adamant to win back Jerusalem he penned a manual, *De recuperatione Terrae Sanctae* (*The Recovery of the Holy Land*). Philippe de Mézières (c. 1327-1405), a Renaissance man before the term or era existed, and contemporary of knight Geoffroi de Charny, obsessed over how to reconquer the Holy Land, rising to become chancellor in Cyprus and contemplating his dream of a military-monastic order, L'Ordre de la Passion du Christ.[6] Philip VI (reigned 1328-1350), whom Geoffroi de Charny served on a variety of military missions, hoped to lead a Holy League to regain the Holy Land – until his conflict with Edward III over succession to the French throne instituted the Hundred Years' War.[7] Amadeus VI of Savoy (1334-1383) desired to actually bring the physical holy sepulcher of Christ itself back to Savoy, build a monastery around it, and end his days.[8]

What Amadeus the Green Count of Savoy hoped to achieve literally was already undertaken symbolically by churches, cathedrals, monasteries, abbeys and convents since the time of Charlemagne (d. 814). Charlemagne's own octagonal Palatine Chapel in Aachen, and the locale where thirty-one German emperors were crowned drew heavily on the Church of the Holy Sepulcher's layout and its octagon aedicule. When St. Louis was developing the Sainte-Chapelle in Paris in the 1240s, he deliberately

---

6 N. Jorga, *Philippe de Mézières, 1327-1405 et La Croisade Au XIV Siecle* (Paris, 1896).

7 See Christopher Tyermann, "Philip VI of France and the Recovery of the Holy Land," in *English Historical Review*, 1985.

8 Eugene L. Cox, *The Green Count of Savoy: Amadeus VI and Transalpine Savoy in the Fourteenth Century* (Princeton: Princeton UP, 1967), 329.

evoked the palatine layout of not only Aachen for his relic depository, but the *Cámara Santa* de Oviedo,[9] a pilgrim station on the Camino de Santiago de Compostela, and home of the "sudarium of Oviedo."[10]

Let us return to Charlemagne's grasp of architectural significance. Johannes Fried summarized Charlemagne's consciousness of the symbolism:

> A predetermined numerical symbolism lay behind the construction of the octagon and the sixteen-sided ambulatory. The proportions of both were determined by the perfect number six and eight, the numeral relating to the resurrection of Christ and of the dead. [...] The diameter of the octagon was 48 feet (six times eight), while that of the sixteen-sided ambulatory was twice that. The total length of the two constructions was three times 48 or 144 feet; 144 was a significant number in numerology, being the number of cubits that St. John ascribed to the periphery of the Holy City of Jerusalem in the book of Revelation (21:17). The circumference of the octagon, measured between the internal corners, was also 144 feet.

Additionally, Fried notes the enthroned Christ surrounded by 144 stars at the top of the chapel's cupola below three rows of arches: "The entire building from top to bottom was proportioned and executed according to figures that related to the End of Days."[11] Charlemagne's architectural choices reflected themes from his favorite book, St. Augustine's *The City of God*.[12]

If one could not journey to Jerusalem, Jerusalem would be brought to them. Such was the case with the eventual rise of the Gothic cathedral. Anonymous master builders seeped in crusader lore, thoroughly shaped by Scripture and a worldview geared towards Final Judgment and the Last

---

9 Pierre Dor, *Les reliquaires de la Passion en France du Ve au XVe siècle* (Amiens: Centre d'archéologie et d'histoire médiévales des établissements religieux (CAHMER), 1999), 107.

10 Championed by sindonologist Fr. Giulio Ricci as the cloth which initially wrapped the face of the crucified Christ prior to burial in the tomb, Ricci detected points of congruency with the face of the man on the Shroud. See his 1976 book, *The Holy Shroud*, 137-143, for a summary on his sudarium of Oviedo hypothesis. Three fragments of the sudarium of Oviedo were sent to C14 labs between 1990 and 1992, each returning a dating between the sixth and ninth centuries. Another test was done in 2007 yielding the same results. See Nicolotti, *The Turin Shroud*, 64n184-185. This dating roughly corresponds with the known historical provenance of the cloth, in the reign of the Oviedo-born king Alfonso II of Asturias (c.760-842), celebrated in Camino de Santiago lore as not only the discoverer of Saint James's tomb, but the trailblazer of the first pilgrim trail of the Camino, from Oviedo to Santiago de Compostela (a route known as Camino Primitivo, the Primitive Way).

11 Johannes Fried, *Charlemagne* (Cambridge: Harvard UP, 2016), 358.

12 A.D. Fitzgerald (ed.), *Augustine through the Ages. An Encyclopedia* (Grand Rapids: Cambridge, 1999), 128.

Days, incorporated the sacred geometry of the Heavenly Jerusalem at the service of their own bishops and dioceses.

At the center of that worldview: Jesus Christ, the ruler of the universe, the Pantocrator, whose face of judgment gazes out at the center of every cathedral rose window. And just as prominent, the namesake of so many Gothic cathedrals – Christ's mother, the *theotokos*, the Mother of God, Christianity's "eternal feminine." A Jesuit priest once utilized the appositive phrase for a poem of the same name, "The Eternal Feminine":

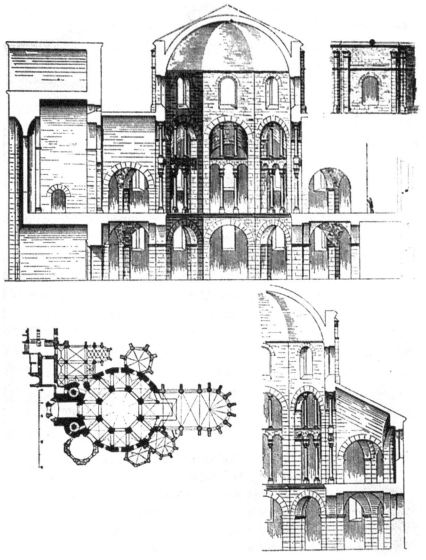

Architectural plans of Charlemagne's Aachen Cathedral, inspired directly by the Holy Sepulcher in Jerusalem

"I am the translucent medium between God and men. It is I who drew the Word down to earth, and it is I whose charm draws the earth to me, that I may give it to God. In me – and not in the flesh – are consummated the nuptials of the world and Creator. I am Mary, the Virgin, the Church."[13]

The author of the poem, Pierre Teilhard de Chardin, was a Jesuit priest, paleontologist, geologist, cosmologist, and veteran of World War I. He was also born in Orcines, France, five miles east of Clermont, where Pope Urban II thunderously spurred knight and noble alike into the First Crusade in 1095. Teilhard grew up in the shadow of Clermont's 13th century Gothic cathedral, its twin spires soaring over 300 feet, and named in honor of Our Lady of the Assumption.

Though constructed over decades, if not centuries for some, the cathedral was an unavoidable part of the landscape in medieval life by its sheer size alone. Florence's landmark cathedral for example, Santa Maria del Fiore, began construction in 1296 but was only completed in 1436. The cathedral centerpiece, Filippo Brunelleschi's dome, is an example of Gothic architecture merging into the early Renaissance. The brick comprising the enormous 375-foot-high dome was assembled in a herringbone pattern to help offset the very real possibility of the dome caving in onto the sanctuary below.

The refashioned cathedrals from Romanesque into the Gothic style served as not only the seat for the local bishop, but became temples for relics, many of them shipped from Outremer and later Constantinople, a tradition dating to the very early centuries of Christianity. Originally a negative term coined by Renaissance artists referring to the "Goths" who ravaged Rome, "Gothic" hearkens back to France's origins as a country, particularly the Ile-de-France area, which encompassed Champagne. William Anderson, in *The Rise of the Gothic*, aptly describes the numerous spiritual components fused into the cathedral, particularly its evocation of the Book of Revelation's Jerusalem:

> Set on a high hill or dominating a plain, it was a future of Jerusalem on earth: it stood for the goal of what was called the Great Pilgrimage, the journey through Egypt and Mount Sinai to Jerusalem, returning to Rome. It was also the image of the Heavenly Jerusalem – as glistening a simulacrum of the Apocalyptic city as human hands could make. The relics it contained, whether portions of Christ's or His

13 Henri de Lubac, *The Eternal Feminine: A Study on the Text of Teilhard de Chardin* (New York: Harper & Row, 1971), 23.

Mother's clothing or instruments of the Passion, or the bones of apostles and of saints of the Dark Ages or of more recent martyrs such as Thomas a Becket, made it a place where miracles were to be expected, where the mortally ill and chronically sick could be cured, where long-cherished desires could be granted, and where special graces in consolation and recollection of the soul might be bestowed.[14]

Indeed, the concept of the Heavenly Jerusalem was so prevalent creators of the Amiens Project at Columbia University noted the presence of literal numerology as depicted in Revelation within the cathedral architecture. Just as Charlemagne intended for his sanctuary, Professor Stephen Murray connected the height of Amiens Cathedral, 144 Roman feet high, with heaven's height as described in Revelation as 144 cubits high. At Notre-Dame in Paris, constructed between 1160 and 1260, medieval builders looked to Chapter Six of the First Book of Kings and its description of Solomon's Temple:

> The house which King Solomon built for the LORD was sixty cubits long, twenty wide, and thirty high.[15]

Notre-Dame's first two levels match these dimensions precisely.

19th c. statue of Charlemagne before Notre-Dame de Paris | Photo by James Day

14 William Anderson, *The Rise of the Gothic* (New York: Dorset, 1988), 158.
15 1 Kings 6:2

Justin A.E. Kroesen noted, "[Medieval Christians] believed that the miraculous power of the original tomb was transferred to a consecrated Holy Sepulchre in Western Europe, so that in this way the Holy Places were also close at hand in the West."[16] Ultimately, in the century after the Mamluks captured Acre, this meant something more than simply recreating the physical Holy Sepulchre or the attainment of relics. What worshipers longed for beyond adoring the empty tomb was nothing less than the body of Christ.

It was something no earthly crusade could achieve.

---

16 J.A.E. Kroesen, *Sepulchrum Domini Through the Ages: Its Form and Function* (Leuven: Peeters Publishers, 2000), 13.

CHAPTER TWO

FAMILY TIES

Like other noble houses, the ancestors of knight Geoffroi de Charny (c. 1300-September 19, 1356) deeply involved themselves with monastic life, indicative of a worldview and lifestyle that itself was largely monastic.[1] Monachism, a little used term today, aptly describes this outlook on life. Jochem Schenk noted, "It was with revenues from [landed families'] estates and with the knights and non-nobles who flocked to their houses that the Templars were able to organize, finance, and maintain a presence in the Latin East for almost two hundred years."[2] The Cistercians, founded by St. Robert of Molesme, were especially connected with Burgundian crusading families. In his study on the founding of Citeaux, Hungarian-born Cistercian Fr. Bede Lackner observed:

> Whenever he (Robert) is on a mission or makes a foundation, from Troyes to Tonnerre, at Molesme or at Citeaux, he is protected and even aided by the prelates and the baronial descendants of the ancient house of *Vergy*, or the Milonides, or the Mainier; hence the Malignys, the viscounts of Beaune, *the lords of Mont-Saint-Jean*, and of Couches were all possibly cousins of the great abbot.[3]

Indeed, one could add the sire of Joinville and Vaucouleurs to Robert's network. Geoffroi II de Joinville, a contemporary of Robert, donated to the abbeys at Vaucouleurs and Molesme.[4] Robert of Molesme and about twenty other Benedictine monks from the widely influential Cluny Monastery, so influential it was only answerable to the Supreme Pontiff, where a cult of the Passion, Marian devotions, and indebtedness to both Celtic monachism and Byzantine art were fostered,[5] and also where the future Pope Urban II was an abbey prior, felt the community had strayed

---

1   See Arnaud Baudin, *The Knights Templar: From the Days of Jerusalem to the Commanderies of Champagne* (Paris: Somogy Editions d'Art), 2013.
2   Jochem Schenk, *Templar Families: Landowning Families and the Order of the Temple in France, c. 1120-1307* (Cambridge: Cambridge UP, 2012), 2.
3   Bede Lackner, *11th Century Background of Citeaux* (Washington: Cistercian Publishers, 1972), 218, emphasis mine.
4   "Sur la Chronologie des sires de Joinville" (Paris: Didot, 1871), 210.
5   See Deno Geanakopols, *Byzantine East & Latin West: Two Worlds in Middle Ages and Renaissance* (New York: Harper Books, 1966).

from authentic adherence to the Rule of St. Benedict. They established a new abbey south of Dijon in the village of Citeaux, and a derivative of the town's name, Cistercian, defined the new order. In the charter of Citeaux's foundation in 1098 prepared by Odo I, Duke of Burgundy, Geoffroi de Charny's ancestor Hugues I de Mont-Saint-Jean is credited as the first lay witness.[6] Hugues II, Geoffroi's paternal great-great-grandfather and lord of Charny, was so involved with Citeaux he is buried with his wife, Elisabeth de Vergy, in a prominent tomb on the abbey's grounds. Thus, the later union of Geoffroi de Charny and his second wife, Jeanne de Vergy, was not the first between the two noble houses. In fact, dating as far back as the tenth century, the two houses were intimately connected, so much so that the house of Mont-Saint-Jean descended from the founder of the Vergy.[7]

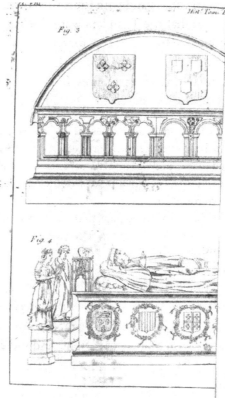

Tomb of Elisabeth de Vergy and Hugues I de Mont-Saint-Jean, both deceased c. 1196, with blasons that will also appear on the later Lirey Shroud Pilgrim Badge (Histoire de l'Academie Royale des Inscriptions et Belles-Lettres t. 9)

---

6   *Histoire de l'Academie Royale des Inscriptions et Belles-Lettres*, t. 9 (Paris, 1736), 201.

7   Jean Mesqui, "Le Chateau de Mont-Saint-Jean" (Paris, 1989) 145.Also Noel Currer-Briggs, *The Holy Grail and the Shroud of Christ* (London: ARA Publications, 1984), 66: "The earliest recorded seigneur of Mont-Saint-Jean was Gollut, who claimed descent from Manasses, the founder of the great castle of Vergy about 880."

Arthur Forgeais, Collection de plombs historiés trouvés dans la Seine, tome IV : Imagerie religieuse. Paris, 1865, p. 105

As detailed in the chapter "A Place of Pilgrimage," the pilgrim badge featuring the Shroud, a piece of which is shown above, details the Charny coat of arms (left, gules with three silver shields) and Vergy coat of arms (right, three cinquefoils). A small distinction is the color of the shields – silver for Charny, but gold for Mont-Saint-Jean.[8]

The family Vergy, one of the most ancient dating back to the Merovingian kingdom of Burgundy in the seventh century, possessed an imposing chateau, below which lay the winemaking Cluniac priory, Abbaye Saint Vivant de Vergy. Geoffroi's relatives were involved with Bussiere, daughter abbey of Citeaux, burial places for the wives of the Burgundian dukes; Pontigny, at the time when Thomas Becket, archbishop of Canterbury, resided for two years while hunted by King Henry II; and Theuley, among others. But Citeaux remained the chief nexus of spiritual and political gatherings. It was the General Chapter at Citeaux in September 1201 where abbots, Burgundian barons and Frankish knights vowed to take the cross fourteen years after Saladin wrested control of Jerusalem and the Latin kingdom relocated north to Acre. Among those in attendance at Citeaux who championed Boniface de Montferrat as the crusade's leader was Guillaume de Champlitte, former husband of Geoffroi

---

8   Ernest Petit, *Histoire des Ducs de Bourgogne*, Tome V (Dijon, 1887), 448.

de Charny's great-great aunt, Elisabeth de Mont-Saint-Jean, and future prince of Achaea.[9]

The Templar Knights, whose commanderies dotted Burgundy and Champagne, home of the order's original knights, also received donations, gifts, and properties from these noble families. Before joining the Templars in Jerusalem, Hugh, count of Champagne and grandfather of the aforementioned Guillaume de Champlitte, donated a land grant in 1115 to Clairvaux Abbey. That same year, a monk from Citeaux named Bernard was ordered to found a new Cistercian abbey in a swamp called Clairvaux. Bernard brought with him thirty relatives to the new house, an early sign of the future doctor of the church's power of persuasion.

Bernard of Clairvaux's father, Tescelin le Roux, was a Burgundian knight who married Aleth de Montbard, venerated as a saint in the Catholic Church. Aleth's brother, André de Montbard, was one of the original nine Poor Fellow-Soldiers of Christ and of the Temple of Solomon, the Knights Templar. Bernard of Clairvaux played a central role in legitimizing the new military order in the eyes of the papacy. Bernard contributed a number of writings about the order's rule, such as *Specific Behavior for the Templar Order*, and most notably, *In Praise of New Knighthood* (*Liber ad milites templi de laude novae militiae*). The rule, which stipulated the Templar knights to take monk-like vows of poverty, chastity, and obedience, was adopted at the Council of Troyes in January 1129. A series of papal bulls issued by various pontiffs in the succeeding years provided the Templars with extraordinary range of operations; by the mid-12th century, the Templars would already be scaling the heights of military prowess, wealth, and regional influence with the construction of their imposing military fortifications situated in strategic locations.

These men from Champagne took their monastic vows before the Latin Patriarch of Jerusalem, Warmund of Picquigny, at the Church of the Holy Sepulchre, vowing to defend the Christian pilgrimage route into Jerusalem. King Baldwin II of Jerusalem (reigned 1118-1131), a native of Rethel outside Reims and crusader under his relative Godfrey of Bouillon in the First Crusade, was instrumental in establishing the Templars in Jerusalem. It was a structure on the Temple Mount in the shadow of the Dome of the Rock where Baldwin II housed Hugues de Payens and the other founding members of the Templars. This site was deemed in the crusader period *Templum Solomonis*, Solomon's Temple, believing the original temple destroyed by

---

9   Geoffroi Villehardouin, *De la Conquête de Constantinople*, trans. Frank Marzials. (New York: Dutton, 1872), 12.

the Babylonians was underneath. The Dome of the Rock became the *Templum Domini*, a church maintained by Augustinians.

Eventually brought down by Philip IV of France in the first decade of the fourteenth century, the Templars until that moment enjoyed rapid expansion from the Middle East into England. The Templars generated a mystique around them that stirred the imagination of Christian poets and troubadours already intoxicated by the exotic notion of crusade and the apocalyptic symbolism fashioned by the Kingdom of Jerusalem. In their waning years, charges of heresy, blasphemy and idolatry would be leveled against the order amid a highly controversial Grail-like object of veneration, a "head," likened by some as the mandylion, if not the Shroud of Turin.[10]

While the Templars were disbanded by the time Geoffroi de Charny came of age, we see as their legacy vestiges of devoutness towards Jerusalem and the person of Jesus Christ. The Cistercians; the Carthusians, established by St. Bruno in 1084; the Order of Canons Regular of Prémontré, the Norbertines, established near Laon in 1120; and the Franciscans, established in 1209, all emerged out of the same spiritual milieu of identifying with Christ by uniting one's sorrows with the suffering of Christ.

* * *

Yet long before the medieval period, this region of France, anchored by Troyes, was destined as a place of profound events. Attila the Hun (d. AD 453) even attempted to control Roman Gaul, which Julius Caesar had conquered upon defeating Gaul's Vercingetorix in 46 BC. Attila's campaign climaxed at the Battle of the Catalaunian Plains on June 20, 451. This battle occurred somewhere between the city of Troyes and Châlons-Sur-Marne. The conflict involved numerous affiliations on both sides, including the local Germanic peoples called the Salian Franks, fighting for the Roman Empire. Among the Franks participating in the battle under the leadership of Roman general Flavius Aetius was likely a young man named Childeric, whose future military accomplishments in the region would set the stage for the Merovingian dynasty, which would come into its own under Childeric's son, Clovis I, the first Catholic king of the Franks.

Clovis was only 15 when he succeeded his father, Childeric, as Merovingian king in 481. The spiritual landscape of the Franks at the time of Clovis's rise broadly consisted of a hybridization of pagan Germanic

---

10 See Barbara Frale, for one: *The Templars and the Shroud of Christ* (New York: Skyhorse Publishing, 2012).

myths and Greco-Roman mythology and tradition. A founding myth for the Franish people told of refugees after the fall of Troy settling in Sicambria in eastern Europe and gradually making their way westward.

Clovis spent the next thirty years until his death in battle, subjugating regional sub-kings such as the Visigoths' Alaric II, whose defeat at Vouille near Poitiers brought Toulouse and Aquitaine under Frankish control; other conquests included Soissons, the Thuringian campaign into modern eastern Germany; Dijon, whose ruler, Gondebald the King of the Burgundians and brutal uncle of Clovis's wife, surrendered to Clovis at Avignon in 500; and Strasbourg. By 508, Clovis ruled all Franks under one kingdom, Francia, and made Paris his primary residence. A convert to the faith largely fueled by the influence of his wife, the Burgundian princess St. Clotilde, Clovis established his empire in full communion with Rome, so much so he earned the nickname the "Most Christian King" by the pope.

The time of Clovis corresponded with that of Saint Benedict, with both setting the stage for the renewal of western civilization. Yet, in the East, Christianity and the Roman Empire endured in Byzantium, where Constantine in the fourth century relocated the seat of the empire from Rome and renamed it Constantinople. The shift isolated the pope, a spiritual and temporal leader with little influence.

Constantinople even tried to wield its own claim to apostolic supremacy. Twentieth century historian Henri Marrou noted: "Taking advantage of the presence of St. Andrew's relics, which had been brought to the city by the Emperor Constantius in 357, Constantinople worked out the legend of a pretended apostolic origin, with the idea of establishing perfect equality with Rome, if not even a vague supremacy over the Western city."[11]

---

11 Henri Marrou, "The Great Persecution to the Emergence of Medieval Christianity" in *The Christian Centuries, Volume I: The First Six Hundred Years*, ed. Marrou and Jean Daniélou (New York: Paulist Press, 1964), 393.

CHAPTER THREE

A DRAMA UNFOLDS

I f the builder of the church of the Holy Sepulchre, Constantine, as well as his Byzantine Empire in Constantinople stoked the Christian flame throughout the East, it was the Order of Saint Benedict that pulled western Christendom out of the Dark Ages. By establishing the first Benedictine monastery at Monte Cassino in 529, over a temple of Apollo, over the ruins of the Roman town Casinum, Benedict (c. 480-550) was reconstituting pagan Rome into fortifications of the Christian west.

"Benedict, like Abraham, became the father of many nations," Joseph Cardinal Ratzinger stated at Subiaco, where St. Benedict, as a teenager, lived in a cave for three years honing the foundation of his Benedictine Rule.[1] When he emerged a hermit no more, the age of monasticism began. It is the Benedictines to whom the Cistercians, Carthusians, Norbertines, and Franciscans owe much. By 817, Louis the Pious, son of Charlemagne, decreed that all monasteries throughout the Holy Roman Empire employ the Rule of St. Benedict.[2]

The commemoration of Christ's passion, death, and resurrection infused Benedictine rituals, particularly in visual allusions to Christ's death and placement in the tomb: A funeral pall was placed over each new Benedictine inductee. The shedding of old clothes in favor of new ones symbolized a dying of an old life to a new one. This motif continues with catechumens baptized into the Catholic Church on Holy Saturday: one's old life is represented by a sack cloth, new linen robes welcome one into the light of faith.[3]

The English Catholic kings of the tenth century, such as King Edgar (d. 975), saw St. Benedict's Rule as a way to revitalize monasticism in England.[4] One of the chief proponents of English Benedictine reform was St. Æthelwold, bishop of Winchester. St. Æthelwold is credited for compiling an appendix for English use of the Rule of St. Benedict, called the *Regu-*

---

1   Joseph Ratzinger, "Europe's Crisis of Cultures," Lecture delivered on April 1, 2005.
2   George Klawitter, "Dramatic Elements in Early Induction Ceremonies" in *Comparative Drama*, Vol. 15, Fall 1981, 213-220.
3   Ibid.
4   Julia Barrow, "The Chronology of the Benedictine Reform" in *Edgar, King of the English 959-975*, ed. Donald Scragg (Woodbridge: Boydell Press, 2008), 211-213.

laris Concordia.[5] For our purposes here, the *Regularis Concordia* is an early example of the Easter liturgical drama, particularly the *Visitatio Sepulchri* (Visit to the Tomb) sequence.[6] This manuscript from Winchester joins other such texts as those from St. Gall and Limoges with similar Easter liturgical drama rubrics.

Here, at the dawn of post-classical Roman drama, the Holy Sepulchre takes center stage.[7] David Bjork noted the Visitatio Sepulchri developed from the *Quem Quaeritis* trope that constituted the Easter *Introit* prayer, here taken from the tenth century manuscript of St. Gall:

> Interrogatio. Quem quaeritis in sepulchro, o Christicolae?
>
> Whom do you seek in the tomb, O followers of Christ?
>
> *Responsio. Jesum Nazarenum crucifixum, o caelicolae.*
>
> Jesus of Nazareth the crucified, o heavenly beings.
>
> *Angeli. Non est hic; surrexit, sicut praedixerat. Ite, nuntiate quia surrexit de sepulchro*
>
> The Angels: He is not here; he is risen, just as he foretold. Go, announce that he is risen from the sepulchre.[8]

St. Æthelwold's stage directions for the scene – which was enacted at Matins on Easter morning – dictates clerics, as the Three Marys (myrrhbearers):

> ...vested in copes, bearing in their hands thuribles with incense, and stepping delicately as those who seek something, approach the sepulchre. These things are done in imitation of the angel sitting in the monument, and the women with spices coming to anoint the body of Jesus. When therefore he who sits there beholds the three approach him like lost folk and seeking something, let him begin in a dulcet voice of medium pitch to sing Quem quaeritis. And when he has sung it to the end, let three reply in unison Ihesu Nazarenum. So he, Non est hic, surrexit sicut praedixerat. Ite, nuntiate quia surrexit a mortuis. At the word of this bidding let those three turn to the choir and say Alleluia! Resurrexit Dominus! This said, let the one, still sitting there and as if recalling them say the anthem Venite et videte locum. And saying this, let him rise, and lift the veil, and show them the place bare of the cross, but only the

---

5   E.K. Chambers, *The Medieval Stage, Vol. II* (Oxford: Oxford UP, 1903), 14.

6   David A Bjork,. "On the Dissemination of *Quem quaeritis* and the Visitatio sepulchri and the Chronology of Their Early Sources" in *Comparative Drama*, vol. 14 no. 1, 1980, 46-69.

7   Aballéa, "Introduction," par. 5.

8   John Gassner, ed. *Medieval and Tudor Drama* (New York: Applause, 1987), 35.

cloths laid there in which the cross was wrapped. And when they have seen this, let them set down the thuribles which they bare in that same sepulchre, and take the cloth, and hold it up in the face of the clergy, and as if to demonstrate that the Lord has risen as is no longer wrapped therein, let them sing the anthem Surrexit Dominus de sepulchro, and lay the cloth upon the altar.[9]

The exposition of the cloth from the tomb by the Three Marys here in the Visitatio Sepulchri is echoed later in devotions from the Holy Grave and Entombment monuments to the cult of Veronica's Veil and clerical ostensions of the Shroud of Turin. Donna Sadler remarked, "[A]t the same moment the *Quem quaeritis* drama was being enacted in the tenth and eleventh century, there were a number of visual representations of the angel pointing to the empty shroud as the Holy Women gaze at the vacant tomb."[10] The visual element of abandoned burial cloths conveyed without the need for wordy explanations or theological discourse that something remarkable and transformative occurred in the tomb.

Angel points to the burial cloths, illustration in Hartker's Liber responsalis (Responsory Book), St. Gall

9 Chambers, 14-15.
10 Donna L. Sadler, *Stone, Flesh, Spirit: The Entombment of Christ in Late Medieval Burgundy and Champagne* (Leiden: Brill, 2015), 73.

Above an image from Psalter of Frederick II, c. 1235; below, the "White Angel" fresco in the Serbian monastery of Mileševa

In the Resurrection Play of Tours (*Ludus Paschalis*), the Three Marys kiss the shroud before showing the sudarium and burial shroud.[11]

---

11 Young, The Drama of the Medieval Church, Vol. I (Oxford: Clarendon Press, 1933), 419.

The *Visitatio Sepulchri* motif is the triumphant moment in the Easter liturgical drama. It follows the *Depositio*, the moment in the Good Friday liturgy when two clerics, representing Joseph of Arimathea and Nicodemus, place either a cross, effigy of Christ, consecrated host, or sometimes, as in the Barking *Depositio*,[12] an image of Christ into a designated part of the church as the sepulchre. There it would remain until the *Elevatio*, when a cleric would remove the object symbolizing the resurrection of Christ, sometime before Matins in the darkness of Easter morning.

Folio 85 in the *Codex Egberti*, an illuminated Gospel book for Egbert, Bishop of Trier, depicts a bare deposition and entombment scene featuring only Joseph of Arimathea and Nicodemus. As both the liturgical dramas and later grave monuments evolved, the more elaborate the proscenium. Compare Folio 85 from the Codex Egberti, c. 980 with the Holy Grave sepulchres from Alsace c. 1330; and the Entombment monument at the chapel of Ste. Croix de Jerusalem at the Dijon hospital of St Espirit c. 1500:

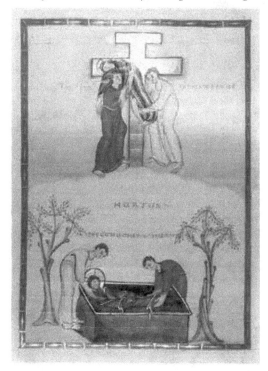

Folio 85, Codex Egberti, reflecting the hastiness of Christ's burial, as it was the day of preparation.[13]

---

12 Neil C. Brooks, *The Sepulcre of Christ in Art and Liturgy* (Champagne: Univ. of Illinois Press, 1921), 39 Ibique in specie Joseph et Nichodemi de ligno deponentes Ymaginem uulnera Crucifixi uino abluant et aqua

13 Cf. Mk 15:42.

Illustration of Holy Sepulchre monument in the church of Saint-Dominique, 14th c. (Adrien Dauzats, d. 1868, Bibliothèque nationale de France)

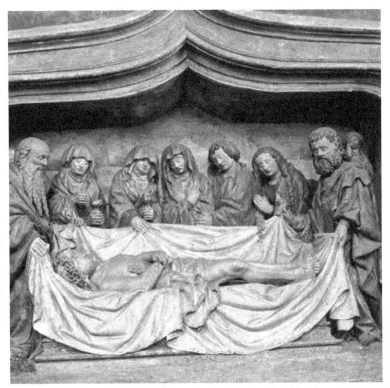

Entombment from the chapel of Ste. Croix de Jerusalem at the Dijon hospital of St Espirit (courtesy Donna L. Sadler)

Lithograph of stained-glass entombment, 1548, Sainte-Chapelle, Chambery during Shroud's stay before moving to Turin (photo by John Beldon Scott, *Architecture for the Shroud* (Chicago: Univ. of Chicago Press, 2003), 44; used with permission

Gabriel Dufour "Le Saint-Suaire" (1668) evoking the mourners in entombment sculptures | Benoît Brassoud / Wikimedia Commons, License CC BY-SA 4.0

By the time of large-scale entombments, those elaborate scenes resembled a wake-like vigil – no longer the sense of urgency of an impromptu burial before Passover – conflating multiple moments (Joseph and Nicodemus, the mourning women, the sleeping guards, the angels) into one frame. In these we see the *pietà* (known as *vesperbild* in its German origins): the mourning, collapsing Mother of God – a scene not mentioned in the Gospels, albeit a visualization of Simeon's prophecy to Mary that "a sword will pierce your heart also".[14]

---

14 Lk 2:35.

Visualization of Simeon's prophecy with the Veil of Veronica | Courtesy Paul Badde

As Donna Sadler points out, "Preoccupation with the moment of Christ's death and with his sufferings dominated late medieval theology and the devotion it fostered."[15] The quest for greater realism can also be seen in developments in Holy Week commemorations of Christ's passion and death, reflecting a broader cultural identification with the Five Wounds of Christ, a devotion honed by monastic orders not least the Franciscans and German mystics, in writings such as *Meditations on the Life of Christ,*[16] and fringe groups such as the Flagellants, Flemish itinerants who sought to spiritually repel the Black Death in 1349 by scourging themselves and were condemned by Pope Clement VI. An eyewitness noted:

---

15 Sadler, 74.
16 Pseudo-Bonaventure, *Meditations on the Life of Christ: An Illustrated Manuscript of the Fourteenth Century,* trans. Isa Raguso and Rosalie Green (Princeton: Princeton UP 1977).

51

Each had in his right hand a scourge with three tails. Each tail had a knot and through the middle of it there were sometimes sharp nails fixed. They marched naked in a file one behind the other and whipped themselves with these scourges on their naked and bleeding bodies.[17]

A rodent-carried disease, the plague first arrived in Europe by way of Italy, reaching Burgundy in July 1348 before creeping into Paris at the end of the summer. Once contracting the disease, victims met a swift but painful death. Some 30% upwards to 60% of Europe's population was killed by it – certainly a third of western Europe's population died. In Avignon in 1348, 1,000 people were buried in a single graveyard in a six-week period.

The suffering of the populace and the religious reawakening it spawned was reflected in images of the suffering, crucified Christ. In the Holy Sepulchre monument in the Alsacian church of Saint-Dominique in Vieux-Thann, the Christ effigy (also called a *gisant*) was one that took on startling human characteristics. Here, the recumbent Christ's gaunt figure reveals his ribcage and popping veins along both arms.[18] At Wienhausen, a Cistercian abbey until the Reformation, a wooden sculpture of a bloodied Christ in death was housed in a moveable sepulchre.

Amy Powell detailed a crucified Christ with hinged joints and moveable arms, a mechanical feat popular at the end of the thirteenth century and into the fourteenth that "stands as the culmination of the medieval development of an increasingly realistic image of the crucified body,"[19] such as the mid-fourteenth century crucifix with moveable arms and a gushing side wound in the Basilica of St. Lorenz in Kempten, a church once nestled amid numerous Benedictine abbeys in the Holy Roman Empire. These sort of "special effects" shocked congregations into empathy with Christ's way of suffering, such as Passion dramatizations that included a lifelike figure "fitted out with human hair and with a hollow in its side through which a bag of animal blood could be pierced with a spear to stimulate the piercing of Christ's side as he hung on the cross."[20]

Women mystics, particularly in modern-day Germany, acted out the Crucifixion not only on Good Friday, but on Fridays throughout the year.

---

17 Robert of Avesbury, *Robertus de Avesbury de Gestis Mirabilbus Regis Edwardi Tertii, Roll Series, 1889*
18 See Monique Fuchs, "Le saint sepulcre de Vieux-Thann," in Arte + architettura in Svizzera, 47/2, 47, 1996.
19 Amy Powell, "A Machine For Souls: Allegory Before and After Trent" in *The Sensuous in the Counter-Reformation Church*, eds. Marcia Hall and Tracy E. Cooper (Cambridge: Cambridge UP, 2013), 273-294.
20 Bob Scribner, "Popular Piety and Modes of Visual Perception in Late-Medieval and Reformation Germany" in *The Journal of Religious History*, Vol. 15, No. 4, December 1989, 456.

Among these was a beguine stigmatic Elizabeth of Spalbeek (c. 1246-1304), from the Herkenrode nunnery in the diocese of Liège. In her study of these Passion performances, Carolyn Muessig related that when Elizabeth was 20 years old, Philip, abbot of Clairvaux, was invited to view such a performance by Elizabeth. "Elizabeth acted out the Passion in seven intervals throughout the day corresponding to the seven canonical hours; on Fridays her performance was often accompanied by the reception of the stigmata."[21]

So moved was Philip he likened Elizabeth of Spalbeek to a new St. Francis of Assisi. Philip went on to write a *Vita* of Elizabeth, and what he details offers a window into the role of an image of Christ in relation to the viewer: "At the start of each canonical hour she gazed upon a panel painted with the image of the crucified Christ. The image moved her from considering the icon of Christ crucified 'to contemplation of the truth.'"[22]

For Philip, Elizabeth was a testament for the non-educated populace to understand the mysteries of the faith, "by her limbs and body, just as if she were a living and visible Veronica, just like a moving picture and animated narrative of redemption."[23]

---

21 Carolyn Muessig, "Performance of the Passion: the enactment of devotion in the later Middle Ages" in *Visualizing Medieval Performance: Perspectives, Histories, Contexts*, ed. Elina Gertsman (Farnham: Ashgate, 2017), 130.
22 Ibid., 131
23 Ibid, 131

Portrait XIXe Jean de Joinville Louis IX Saint Louis Champagne

CHAPTER FOUR

JEAN DE JOINVILLE IN ALSACE

In 1300, Jean de Joinville (1224-1317), the seneschal of Champagne and grandfather of knight Geoffroi de Charny, chaperoned King Philip the Fair's sister, Blanche, into Alsace, the autonomous region between France and the Holy Roman Empire and north of the County of Burgundy and Kingdom of Savoy.[1] Blanche was en route to her wedding with Rudolf of Austria, son of the German king Albert I at Haguenau, sixteen miles north of Strasbourg. A year earlier, in the summer of 1299, Joinville hosted King Philip and Albert at Vaucouleurs, on the estate technically owned by Joinville's brother, Geoffroi, the seigneur of Vaucouleurs.

Vaucouleurs was a common meeting place of kings, dating to 860 when King Charles the Bald convened the Council of Tusey. The meeting of this particular summit in 1299 centered around negotiating a new border.[2] Both monarchs stayed at another Joinville local during this meeting, at Reynel, property brought into the marriage by Joinville's second wife, Alix de Reynel.

Joinville's territorial region and status as de facto governor of Champagne allowed him unfettered access to Alsace; Haguenau was only less than one hundred miles from Vaucouleurs. At this time, however, Alsace was not an entirely pacified place, even if it spurred a thriving economy. Holy Roman emperor Frederick II (1194-1250) and his Hohenstaufen family spent much time in the region (Frederick Barbarossa, the emperor's grandfather, built a castle in Haguenau).[3] It was Frederick II who ratified the suzerainty of Alsace to the bishopric of Strasbourg. The people of Strasbourg took issue with this rule, resulting in ongoing conflicts throughout Alsace. By the time of the start of Bishop Conrad of Lichtenberg's reign (1273-1299), a treaty was established, and the people of Strasbourg effectively governed the day-to-day management of the city.[4]

---

1 Jean de Joinville, "Joinville's Chronicle" in *Memoirs of the Crusades*, trans. F. T. Marzials (New York: E.P. Dutton, 1958), 295.

2 See "Chronique de Guillaume de Nangis" in *Historiens de France*, Book 20 (Charleston: Nabu Press, 2012), 581.

3 Nina Rowe, *The Jew, the Cathedral and the Medieval City* (Cambridge: Cambridge UP, 2014), 229.

4 "Strasburg" in *The Catholic Encyclopedia*, Vol. 14, ed. C.G. Herbermann (New York: The Universal Knowledge Foundation, Inc., 1914).

Construction on Strasbourg's towering Gothic cathedral of Notre-Dame was also underway at this time, with the development of the cathedral's west facade overseen by architect Erwin von Steinbach (1244-1318) and his son, Gerlach (d. 1330). Conrad of Lichtenberg's canopied memorial entombment is still to this day within the Strasbourg Cathedral, in the Chapel of Saint Jean the Baptist, with the *gisant* of Bishop Conrad possibly designed by Erwin von Steinbach himself. A successor to Conrad of Lichtenberg, Bishop Berthold II of Bucheck (1328-1353), supported the construction of the cathedral's Saint Catherine Chapel, built circa 1345-1349. Charlotte Stanford noted Bishop Berthold's own planned tomb morphed into a Holy Grave monument by his own initiative. It was a decision that launched "a program of liturgical Easter sculpture in a sepulchral context, for the benefit of the lay congregation."[5] These remarkably Shroud-like effigies of Christ punctuated chapels throughout Alsace beginning in the mid-fourteenth century. They were also a phenomenon unique to the region of Alsace.

Representation of the Holy Sepulcher, 14th c., Saint-Florentius, Niederhaslach, Alsace | Pethrus, CC BY-SA via Creative Commons

5   Charlotte Stanford, "From Bishop's Grave to Holy Grave: The Construction of Strasbourg Cathedral's St. Catherine Chapel" in *Gesta*, Vol. 46, No. 1, (2007), 59.

The Holy Graves, or *heiliges grab* in German, were simple monuments. Generally, Christ lay recumbent in the position of death just as seen on the Shroud and the Three Marys from the canonical Gospels (Mary Magdalene, the Blessed Virgin Mary, and Mary Salome) stand behind the crucified, joined on occasion by an angel or two. Additional characters such as Joseph of Arimathea and Nicodemus only feature in the later and more elaborate Entombments of the fifteenth and sixteenth centuries that dominated France, Burgundy, Italy, and elsewhere. These were distinct to the earlier Holy Grave monuments.

Sylvie Aballéa distinguished two Holy Grave setups within churches and cathedrals: the mobile statuary featuring a carved life-size Christ figure and the permanent monumental tombs. "On the banks of the Rhine, the most important monumental tombs were erected in Basel, then, along the river on the left bank, in Strasbourg, Niederhaslach, Saverne and Haguenau; on the right, in Freiburg im Breisgau and Neuenburg-am-Rhein."[6] Both factored into the perennial Holy Week and Easter liturgies. Both also evoked what remained physically so far away, if not indefinitely unreachable: the Holy Sepulchre itself in Jerusalem.

It is also helpful to mention the sheer prominence of the faith in this area. In 14th century Freiburg, for instance, thirty churches served a population of under ten thousand.

Did someone traveling in Jean de Joinville's retinue take particular notice of the proliferation of images showing the body of Christ in the grave? Was an idea planted that would become the linen cloth known as the Shroud of Turin? Or was it bequeathed to the Joinville entourage as a gift?

A bit further into Swabia we find emerging at this same time depictions of Veronica and her veil on which is shown the face of Christ gazing back at the viewer. The character of Veronica will return throughout this study, but for now, only about a hundred miles from Strasbourg, we find examples of the icon all strategically placed in relation to the sacrament of the Holy Eucharist. At the church of St. Urban, for instance, in Schwabisch Hall, Veronica with her cloth and flanked by two angels appears in an ambry above the grille to the tabernacle (or "sacrament house"). We will also see images such as these vested angels return when exploring Orthodox liturgies and the participation of angels-deacons in the Celestial Liturgy. And just as with other thematic visuals that will emerge, these vested angels were "possibly adopted from Flemish or Burgundian art."[7]

It is to this Holy Face we now turn.

6   Sylvie Aballéa, "Introduction" in *Les saints sépulcres monumentaux: Du Rhin supérieur et de la Souabe (1340-1400)* (Strasbourg: Presses universitaires de Strasbourg, 2003), 9-25.

7   Achim Timmerman, *Staging the Eucharist: Late Gothic Sacrament Houses in Swabia and the Upper Rhine. Architecture and Iconography*. Thesis submitted for the title of Doctor of Philosophy, University of London Courtauld Institute of Art, (1996), 247.

PART II
THE FACE OF GOD

"The Pope Innocent III" - fresco mid 13th century - Monastery of Sacro Speco of Saint Benedict - Subiaco (Rome)

CHAPTER FIVE

INNOCENT III AND THE HOLY FACE

E lizabeeth of Spalbeek flourished at Liège in the years after Norber-
tine canoness Saint Juliana (d. 1258) influenced the Archdeacon
of Liège and future Patriarch of Jerusalem and later Pope Urban
IV, Jacques Pantaleon, to institute the Feast of Corpus Christi in 1264. At
the center of western devotion, beyond the tangible city of Jerusalem and
the Holy Sepulchre, was the manifestation of Christ in the Eucharist. By
its nature, the Body of Christ transcended all relics. The Mass, the central
prayer in Catholicism, itself is the Sacrifice of Christ – with Christ as both
Priest and *Hostia*, sacrificial victim – the Host.

The part of the Mass known as the Consecration is when the priest
"utters the formulae of consecration, and is the agent through whom the
sacrificial act is accomplished."[1] Bread and wine, elements from the Last
Supper, transubstantiate into the Real Presence – the body, blood, soul
and divinity of the resurrected and glorified Second Person of the Trinity – as Christ instructed at the Last Supper: in Latin, *Hoc est enim corpus
meum*...in English, *This is my body*. A pietà from c. 1300-1325, the *Röttgen
Pietà*, visually connects the Eucharist wine with the blood of the crucified
Christ by depicting Christ's blood wounds as grapes. Pope Innocent III
himself wrote, "Water becomes wine, just as the result of Mercy is given
shape by the disposition of Charity."[2]

Transubstantiation was formalized as doctrine in 1215 at the Fourth
Lateran Council by Innocent III (d. 1216). We see in the *Visitatio Sepulchri* how Christ's sarcophagus is reflected in the placement of the linen
graveclothes by the Three Marys on the altar after unveiling them, linking
the altar linens for liturgies with the linen from the tomb. "We may think
of Him on the altar, as if He were placed in the sepulcher," Theodore of
Mopsuestia (d. 428) observed.[3] The altar positioned against the east wall
of churches, towards the rising sun and dawn of resurrected life, as well as

---

1 Young, 18.
2 Innocent III, "Dominica Prima Post Epiphaniam," in *Sermones de Tempore* (n. 26), col. 350.
3 *Commentary of Theodore of Mopsuestia on the Lord's prayer and on the sacraments of baptism and
the eucharist, trans.* Alphonse Mingana (1933), 86.

its stone material and its long surface resembling a bier, further associates the altar with the sepulchre.

Innocent III also reigned as pope during the Fourth Crusade (1202-1204), the detoured campaign led by Boniface of Montferrat that bogged itself down in having to repay debt owed to the Venetians and aiding Byzantine emperor Alexios IV Angelos (8/1203 -1/1204), whose sister, Irene, was married to Boniface's cousin, Philip of Swabia, king of Germany.

Over the Christmas festivities of 1201, Boniface met Alexios IV and was told by the young Greek that vengeance never sleeps – he yearned to unseat his uncle, Alexios III, who blinded his own brother and Alexios IV's father, Isaac II, to claim the Byzantine throne. For his part, however, Boniface knew his primary purpose was to restore Jerusalem to Christendom. But his brother's awful death by poison and the massacre of his own people in Constantinople loomed in Boniface's mind, gradually steering him towards wading deeper into Byzantine family politics.

Meanwhile, the niggardliness of the Byzantine empire had exasperated the powerful Venetians, who were still owed gold from the days of Manuel I. The Republic of Venice at this time lay in the beloved, venerable hands of Enrico Dandolo, the doge of Venice, who by 1201 was nearly 95 years old and like Isaac II, himself blind. Indeed, it is believed the doge was blinded in Constantinople thirty years earlier, sowing seeds of vengeance against Byzantium. Boniface and others met with the doge in 1202 to negotiate Venetian ships transport crusaders to Egypt, and a deal was struck that amounted to the construction by Venice shipbuilders of 60 long ships, 110 dromons, and over 70 other ships. Additionally, Venetians outfitted armor for 1,000 cavalry and 30,000 foot soldiers and crossbowmen. However, reality proved otherwise: less than half the planned crusaders arrived in Venice to the outrage of the Venetians. The doge then suggested the crusaders repay the debt by seizing Zara in Croatia from the Kingdom of Hungary to be brought under Venetian control. Already the plans for the Fourth Crusade were unraveling, and yet knowing Zara was a Catholic state and against the condemnation of Pope Innocent III, Boniface agreed, successfully besieging Zara for two weeks until it capitulated to the Venetians. That Alexios, son of Isaac, was present with the crusaders suggests that Constantinople, not Egypt nor Jerusalem, was always at the forefront of crusade leadership.

Following the successful siege, Innocent III indeed implemented excommunication on the crusaders. But it was at Zara where Alexios IV offered to pay the rest of the outstanding debt owed to the Venetians, even going so far as to promise Christian unity between the East and West – now nearly 150 years since the Great Schism – in exchange for crusader aid in claiming the throne. Nonplussed, Boniface agreed, and in May 1203 the sprawling crusader fleet set off for the Sea of Marmara. The action again stirred Innocent III to respond with an order to avoid Constantinople altogether, though hearing of Alexios IV's promise to unify the splintered Christian world, Innocent relented.

The crusaders reached the shores of Constantinople on July 11, 1203 and were soon met with a defense from Emperor Alexius III. As the fleet sailed around the city into the Bosphorus, the entrance to the Golden Horn was blocked by a sea gate. The crusaders besieged the Tower of Galata where the Byzantines held the gate, but it was broken through and the Byzantines retreated. At that moment, on July 13, Boniface and the leadership ushered Alexios IV into the city, as if a homecoming for the legitimate emperor. Instead, his presence was met with indifferent fanfare from the inhabitants. That Alexios IV was not immediately welcomed and heralded as the rightful heir to the throne clued Boniface and other crusaders into a shocking realization: Alexios IV's promises were vacuous at best, if not utterly deceitful. The city did not desire another emperor. Boniface, feeling duped, fumed as the hordes of crusaders, Venetians, the doge, and others languished unwelcomed outside the ancient walls of Byzantium.

Hell thus enraptured Constantinople. For the next week, the crusaders assaulted the city's defenses with such malice it seemed the entire city would be pulverized as if the ghost of Carthage had descended on the Rome of Constantine. A cowering, fearful Alexius III quaked in the imperial palace until eventually fleeing into Thrace. During this madness, Isaac II, the blinded and former emperor was hoisted up as the emperor once again, along with his wife Margaret-Maria as empress, to the surprise of the crusaders and the chagrin of Alexios IV. Boniface, desperate to get Alexios onto the throne in order for his promises to be made, convinced Isaac II to allow his son to be co-emperor. It was a failed attempt at appeasement. The situation of father and son as co-emperors only incensed the residents of the city to where riots were daily throughout the rest of 1203. On the other hand, the incompetence of the emperors and lack of payment to the Latins resulted in the crusaders setting fires and starting their own riots.

The nightmarish situation in Constantinople only worsened at the turn of 1204. A relatively unknown member of the Byzantine court, a usurper named Doukas, and one unfriendly to the looming presence of the Latin crusaders, locked the emperors in the Blachernae Palace and strangled Alexios IV to death. Isaac II died shortly thereafter by shock. Doukas Mourtzouphlos now became the unlikely emperor Alexios V. It was a reign that would last a couple of months, for the crusaders were now mobilized to sack the city for themselves and install one of their own.

With the city in chaos and the emperorship a vacuum, crusaders could not have anticipated that the sight before them of hallowed Byzantium was in such a state of shambles. At the same time, however, never had such an influential cohort of Latin noblemen as the one now camped at Galata had been as close to the sacred relics that so haunted their ancestors as they were now. It was also the best way to shore up the needed food, supplies, and coin the armies of the west woefully lacked.

A Latin noble, Baldwin of Flanders, was elected over Boniface de Montferrat and installed as the new emperor, at the Hagia Sophia on May 16, 1204 – a Catholic in the center of Orthodoxy – and the Latin Empire of Constantinople was established. Not to be outdone, Boniface took the widowed empress of Constantinople and step-mother of Alexios IV, Margaret of Hungary, as his new bride.

Boniface, his new wife, members of her court, and Boniface's knights set out from Constantinople eastward, where they gradually subdued the sprawling region against local Greek magnates, such as at the Battle of the Olive Grove of Kountouras in the Peloponnese, and the eventual conquest of the second-largest city of the empire, Thessalonika. As if a reincarnated Alexander the Great, Boniface crowned himself king of what he himself dubbed the Kingdom of Thessalonika in 1205. It was a territory that spanned the whole of the empire east of the Bosphorous, down to the Peloponnese in southern Greece.

Vassals of Boniface, among them Guillaume de Champlitte and Geoffroi de Villehardouin, set out to conquer the Peloponnese, establishing the principality of Achaea in 1205. Sixteen baronies were ultimately created in Achaea. In 1316, two baronies were given by Duke Louis of Burgundy to his knight, Dreux de Charny, the brother of Geoffroi de Charny.

* * *

Historian Jean Longon, expert on the Frankish presence in Greece, noted:"[Villehardouin] sent to France, mainly to Champagne, for young knights to occupy the newly conquered lands and the fiefs of those who had returned to the west. Women also came out to settle in the Morea [Achaea], where they founded French families. And gradually there grew up in Greece a chivalric society renowned for its nobility and its refinement."[4]

It was something of sweet revenge for Boniface: it was revenge for the death of his brother, Renier de Montferrat, who was once promised the land years earlier. Renier, son-in-law to Emperor Manuel I, found himself entangled in a Byzantine power struggle after the emperor's death. The chaos eventually resulted in a massacre of Latin inhabitants of Constantinople in 1182, including the decapitation of the papal nuncio to Constantinople, his head dragged through the streets by the tail of a dog, and the strangulation of the imprisoned empress, Maria of Antioch, Manuel I's widow.

The ceaseless cycle of violence dismayed Innocent III. The pontiff was further aghast in the plundering of Constantinople's opulent churches, shrines, and palaces.[5] The aged bishop of Troyes, Garnier de Trainel, uncle by marriage to the powerful duchess of Burgundy, Alix de Vergy, was initially charged with dispersing Constantinople's relics back to the west. It was an ignoble and tragic event, fostering bitterness for centuries into our own time. In greeting ecumenical patriarch Bartholomew I of Constantinople at the Vatican in 2004, Pope John Paul II acknowledged the sins of the past:

> On this journey, we have certainly been oppressed by the memory of the painful events in our past history. In particular, on this occasion we cannot forget what happened during the month of April 1204. An army that had set out to recover the Holy Land for Christendom marched on Constantinople, took it and sacked it, pouring out the blood of our own brothers and sisters in the faith. Eight centuries later, how can we fail to share *the same indignation and sorrow* that Pope Innocent III expressed as soon as he heard the news of what had happened? After so much time has elapsed, we can analyze the events of that time with greater objectivity, yet with an awareness of how difficult it is to investigate the whole truth of history.[6]

---

4   Jean Longon, "The Frankish States in Greece," in *The Later Crusades, 1189-1311*, ed. Kenneth Setton, et al (Madison: University of Wisconsin Press, 1969), 240.

5   Tyerman, *God's War*, 555.

6   John Paul II, "To the Ecumenical Patriarch Bartholomew I," June 29, 2004, http://www.vatican.va/content/john-paul-ii/en/speeches/2004/june/documents/hf_jp-ii_spe_20040629_bartholomew-i.html.

(Above) Stained-glass windows in the Troyes Cathedral (c. 1240-1250) depict the translation of relics from Constantinople, including Garniel de Trainel here holding a vase from Cana (courtesy Painton Cowen, the Medieval Stained Glass Photographic Archive)

(Above) King Louis IX transports the Crown of Thorns reliquary with his brother, Robert d'Artois, into the Sainte-Chapelle. Louis purchased the Passion relics from his relative, Latin emperor Baldwin II of Constantinople, in about 1240

(Above) King Philippe VI and wife, Blanche of Navarre, venerate the Passion relics in the Sainte-Chapelle; from illustrated manuscript by Jean le Noir, Hours de Jeanne de Navarre (c. 1336-1340)

The sacking of Constantinople is where a number of Shroud scholars believe the cloth venerated today in Turin was removed from the imperial church's Pharos Treasury and ushered out of the city.[7] One wonders, then, why the Shroud wasn't returned by the pope to Bartholomew I in 2004 when the stolen relics of St. John Chrysostom and St. Gregory Nazanien were returned. In any case, the usual culprit of this purported Shroud theft is identified as Burgundian knight Othon de la Roche, a follower of Boniface de Montferrat, who founded the duchy of Athens and became its first lord. He fortified the Acropolis, where the Church of Notre-Dame was erected in 1209 and where Latin emperor Henri of Hainaut visited during his imperial tour. de la Roche also dismissed the Orthodox monks from Athens, replacing them with Cistercians from his home fief. Daphni Monastery, for instance, with its striking Christ Pantocrator, was put under the custody of Cistercian monks from Bellevaux Abbey in 1211, a monastery intimately associated with the de la Roches. Othon's uncle was its first abbot.

Christ Pantocrator in the apse of the church at Daphni Monastery, burial locale for the dukes of Athens | Creative Commons, CC BY-SA 4.0 via Wikimedia Commons

---

7   For instance, Gerard Barbet, *Othon de La Roche: chroniques sur l'étonnante histoire d'un chevalier comtois devenu seigneur d'Athènes* (Besançon: Fortis, 2012).

The basis for Othon de la Roche possessing the Shroud comes from a purported letter written to Pope Innocent III from one Theodore Angelos, brother of Michael, Despot of Epirus. Theodore Angelos's letter, dated August 1, 1205, complains to the pope about the Latin treatment of Constantinople's wealth of sacred relics:

> The Venetians partitioned the treasures of gold, silver, and ivory while the French did the same with the relics of the saints and the most sacred of all, the linen in which our Lord Jesus Christ was wrapped after his death and before the resurrection. We know that the sacred objects are preserved by their predators in Venice, in France, and in other places, the sacred linen in Athens.[8]

The letter as an authentic document is in serious question, with only a supposed Latin translation from the 19th century.[9] Suffice it to say for our purposes there exists no other corroborating information about such a letter, or evidence of any reply from Pope Innocent. And while there is ample documentation of correspondence between Pope Innocent and Othon de la Roche in the official files of Innocent III, as well as with Innocent's successor, Honorius III, there is neither a mention of a shroud nor Theodore Angelos' complaint about one.[10]

On the second Sunday after Epiphany in 1208, Innocent III led a barefoot procession of the *sudarium Christi*, an icon retained in St. Peter's. The procession wound from St. Peter's Basilica to the Hospital of the Holy Spirit in Sassia. Innocent specified such a procession to be undertaken yearly.[11] An image of the procession is preserved in the Italian

8 Noel Currer-Briggs, *The Shroud and the Grail: A Modern Quest for the True Grail* (London: Weidenfeld and Nicolson), 147. The rest of the hypothesis usually follows the narrative that Othon de la Roche handed off the Shroud to his father, Pons de la Roche (others say it was kept in the Castle of Ray in Haute-Saone), who in turn handed it off to the St. Etienne cathedral in Besançon. After a fire in 1349, the Shroud was rescued and somehow got to Geoffroi de Charny.

9 See Andrea Nicolotti, "Su alcune testimonianze del Chartularium Culisanense, sulle false origini dell'Ordine Costantiniano Angelico di Santa Sofia e su taluni suoi documenti conservati presso l'Archivio di Stato di Napoli" in Giornale di storia 8 (2012). Also, G. Barbet (see n.60, above) claims de la Roche showed the Shroud to Latin Emperor Henri de Hainaut in Athens in 1209, citing a typed undated document from a Professor Michaelides preserved in the "library of Athens" (102n30). Barbet, likely referring to George Michaelides, does not reproduce the document in his book, which I consulted (D.S. Crawford, *Papyri Michaelidae: being a catalogue of the Greek and Latin papyri, tablets and ostraca in the Library of Mr. G.A. Michaïlidis of Cairo* (1955). I contacted the National Library of Greece in June 2019 but they had no record of such a document. A representative from Fortis, Barbet's publisher, Lydie Joan, acknowledged to me Barbet was likely confused. Filip Van Tricht of Ghent University confirmed in a September 2019 email to me that the only source available for Emperor Henri's 1209 visit to Athens is in Valenciennes, *Histoire de l'empereur Henri de Constantinople*, which does not mention Othon de la Roche exhibiting a shroud.

10 See Innocent III, Opera Omnia, I-IV (PL, 214-217) 215 col. 1270sq; 345f (sermon).

11 Ibid., "Ad commemorandus nuptias," dated January 3, 1208, *Regesta Pontificum Romanorum inde ab a. post Christum natum 1198 ad a. 1304*, trans. A. Potthast.

State Archives featuring Innocent III displaying the face cloth encased in a monstrance, a manner akin to future Corpus Christi processions. Petrus Mallius, a canon of St. Peter's, writing about 1160, specifies the Veronica's location in St. Peter's was in a chapel of the Virgin Mary, next to the chapel of John VII. "As it is attested by oral tradition, Christ wiped off his Holy Face with it before his Passion, when his sweat became like drops of blood flowing to the ground."[12]

While an accepted character in Christian tradition, the Gospels do not attest to a St. Veronica with a veil. She is, however, a character in sixth century or later texts, *The Avenging of the Savior* and *The Death of Pilate*, the later medieval texts, *Gospel of Nicodemus* and a sequence in *The Golden Legend*, and is featured prominently in Christian strands of Arthurian Grail sagas, as we will see. English watercolor painter Thomas Heaphy (1775-1835) wrote in his work *The Likeness of Christ*, "[T]he name of Saint Veronica may be nothing more than a transformation of the words vera icon, or true image."[13]

Innocent III displays the sudarium Christi encased in a monstrance, a manner akin to future Corpus Christi processions (Liber Regulae Sancti Spiritus)

This Roman *sudarium Christi*, championed as a direct relic not only from the time of Christ but one that actually possessed some visage of himself, parallels another contemporary Christ cloth not made by human hands, the mandylion in the East. A facecloth icon of Christ was transferred from Islam-controlled Edessa to Constantinople in August

---

12 Petrus Malleus, *Descriptio basilicae Vaticanae aucta atque emendate a Romano presbitero, c. 27, in Codice topografico della Citta di Roma*, Roberto Valentini, Giuseppe Zucchetti eds, vol. 3, Fonti per la storia d'Italia, XC, (Rome, 1946), 420.

13 Thomas Heaphy, *The Likeness of Christ*, ed. Wyke Bayliss (London: Society for Promoting Christian Knowledge, 1886), 54.

944 overseen by General John Kourkas in exchange for two hundred Muslim prisoners. The event is commemorated to this day as a minor feast on the Byzantine calendar, the Translation of the Icon Not Made by Human Hands. It was this icon Archdeacon Gregory Refendarius associated with a cloth Christ used to wipe off his bloody sweat in the Garden of Gethsemane

This mandylion's arrival in Constantinople occurred one century after the second iconoclast controversy, an explosive theological war over the question of religious images. Emperor Leo III, who saw venerating images as idolatrous, first banned the practice of such devotion in 730. But if it was Leo III who set the ban, it was Leo's son, Constantine V, who violently put Leo's edict into action, spearheading the smashing of images and the hunting down of "the venerators of icons," known as *iconodules*. Glorious churches were destroyed, precious art and architecture forever crushed into smithereens. Replacing the icons and objects were bare churches, adorned with a simple cross. Prelates and faithful who refused to submit to the stripping were condemned and put to the sword. For Constantine V and other iconoclasts, it was not the question of the divinity of Christ at issue, but that the images of Jesus did not – and could not – appropriately express such majesty. The iconoclasts saw the danger of the faithful supplanting the icon as itself divine.

After the death of Constantine V, his son Leo IV took a milder stance against iconoclasm, allowing for the return of exiled monks, for instance. But it was Leo's wife, Empress Irene, who sustained the practice of venerating images in her devotions during the suppression. Following Leo's death, as regent for her young son, Constantine VI, the empress led the restoration of relics and icons in churches and re-established communion with Rome, which had condemned iconoclasm as a heresy. However, a second iconoclasm era took hold in 815. Eventually, in 843, the iconoclast controversy was settled, due in large part to another empress supporting images, Empress Theodora. Byzantine coinage minted in 843 featured, on one side, the regent Theodora and her charge, Michael III. The face of Christ from the chest up was pictured on the flip side. The end of iconoclasm, known as the Triumph of Orthodoxy, is a feast celebrated on the first Sunday of Great Lent.

Pope Saint John Paul II identified that the bottom line for the defense of images was the fact of the Incarnation. "Legitimately, therefore," the pontiff said in 1996, "the artist endeavors to *reproduce his face*, helping each other not only with the power of genius, but above all with the inner docility to the Spirit of God."[14]

To commemorate the Triumph of Orthodoxy, Patriarch of Constantinople Photios I commissioned an illuminated manuscript, *The Homilies of Gregory of Nazianus*, for emperor Basil I, c. 880-886. Mary Ann Graeve noted the depiction of the entombment is one of the "earliest known illustrations of the Entombment."[15]

One of the earliest known depictions of the entombment of Christ (right panel) Grégoire de Nazianze, manuscrit dédié à l'empereur Basile Ier le Macédonien; Bibliothèque nationale de France. Département des manuscrits. Grec 510

Byzantine chronicler Nicolas Choniates detailed how the Stone of Unction, the slab venerated as that on which Christ's body was placed for anointing,[16] was brought to Constantinople in 1169 during the reign of emperor Manuel I Komnenos (d. 1180).[17] The Stone of Unction is rife with liturgical and artistic symbolism. We will see its influence in Byzantine epitaphios liturgical cloths. Additionally, Mary Ann Graeve described the typical layout of Christ as lying "on top of the flat oblong stone, face upwards, almost nude in readiness for unction, hands over lap."[18] The slab was a direct Eucharistic reference: "As the tablet over which the sacred flesh and blood are presented, it would represent the Christian altar."[19]

---

14 John Paul II, Angelus, 11 August 1996, https://www.vatican.va/content/john-paul-ii/it/angelus/1996/documents/hf_jp-ii_ang_19960811.html.

15 Mary Ann Greve, "The Stone of Unction in Caravaggio's Painting for the Chiesa Nuova" in *The Art Bulletin* Vol. 40, No. 3 (Sep., 1958), 223n.5.

16 Cf Jn 19:39

17 Graeve, 228.

18 Ibid., 229.

19 Ibid.

During his reign, Manuel I Komnenos proudly showed Latin visitors the Byzantine imperial collection relics that included the mandylion, among them King Louis VII and Eleanor of Aquitaine, and later King Amalric I of Jerusalem, as he made his way within the imperial palace gawking at the gilded bronze trees, replete with bronze birds and bronze lions.[20] Before the Fourth Crusade, it was a diplomatic custom for relics to be sent from the emperor to the west as gifts and gestures of goodwill.[21] J. Langelle, in his chronicle of another shroud of Christ, the Saint Suaire of Compiègne, mentions Empress Irene, mother of Constantine VI, sending relics to Charlemagne's heir, Charles the Bald.[22]

After the Fourth Crusade, that custom gave way to plunder at the hands of westerners themselves. Robert de Clari, whose on-the-ground chronicle of the Fourth Crusade famously includes a ritual in St. Mary of Blachernae wherein:

> And among those other there was another church which was called My Lady Saint Mary of Blachernae, where there was the shroud (sydoines) in which Our Lord had been wrapped, which every Friday raised itself upright so that one could see the form of Our Lord on it, and no one, either Greek or French, ever knew what became of this shroud (sydoines) when the city was taken.[23]

As noted earlier, de Clari's account is often seized as evidence that such an object was what we now know as the Shroud of Turin. Additionally, as Jean-Pierre Martin observed, "no evidence that this lost sydoines which Robert de Clari would therefore have never have been able to see, is actually the same relic as the Shroud."[24]

Even if Clari's shroud was a burial cloth, it was one of many from Constantinople. Count Riant's sprawling and detailed documentation of the dispersion of relics even names one Robert de Clari as bringing

---

20 See John Kinnamos, *Deeds of John and Manuel Comnenus* (New York: Columbia UP, 1976) and

William of Tyre, *Historia rerum in partibus transmarinis gestarum*, lib XX, c XXIII, in *Recueil des historiens des Croisades*, I,985. See also Alexei Lidov, "A Byzantine Jerusalem. The Imperial Pharos Chapel as the Holy Sepulchre" in *Jerusalem as Narrative Space* (Boston: Leiden, 2012), 63-103.

21 Holger A. Klein, "Eastern Objects and Western Desires: Relics and Reliquaries between Byzantium and the West" in *Dumbarton Oaks Papers*, Vol. 58 (2004), 283-314, sp. 290.

22 J. Langelle, *Histoire du S. Suaire de Compiègne*, 1684, 30.

23 Robert de Clari, *The Conquest of Constantinople*, trans. Peter Dembowski (Paris: Champion, 1904), 90.

24 J.P. Martin, "Notes sur le manuscrit de Bruxelles de Garin le Lorrain," in *Convergences medievales*, ed. N. Henrard et al. Brussels: De Boeck and Larcier (2001), 325-326.

a fragment of Christ's burial shroud back home to Picardy, to Corbie abbey.[25]

Before arriving in Constantinople, this mandylion enjoyed a celebrated history in Edessa, according to the apocryphal story when a cloth was sent by Jesus as a gift to King Abgar of Edessa.[26] In the world of Shroud studies, the idea that the Shroud was in fact the mandylion catapulted the Shroud to prominence in the 1970s.[27] Another image of Christ's face predates the mandylion of Edessa, the Image of Camuliana, named after the ancient town in Cappadocia.[28] The military mastermind and Byzantine emperor Heraclius (c. 575-641), employed a Camuliana icon as a military battle standard during his offensive through Asia Minor that culminated in returning the True Cross, by far the most prized relic for crusaders, captured by the Persians in their assault on Jerusalem and the Holy Sepulcher a generation earlier.[29]

The fascinating and complex history of Christianity's devotion to Christ's face on a cloth deserves separate attention independent of this work.[30] However, since the notion of the Shroud is the mandylion (and the mandylion is the Shroud) has taken hold as fact by certain presenters of the Shroud's history, it is required to briefly summarize this idea.

Like the later Grail legends, this, too, features a wounded king. Abgar V Ukkama, who ruled the kingdom of Osroene at its capital city, Edessa in Upper Mesopotamia until about AD 40. At the time, Edessa was a non-Christian Arab land. Yet somehow the remote kingdom morphed into a citadel of early Christianity and became the first kingdom to embrace Christianity. Its transformation is owed to the legendary healing of the ailing King Abgar, who suffered from leprosy and arthritis. In short, this tale inherited layers of additions and modifications throughout time. For instance, at once it is a story about a letter

---

25 Paul Riant, *Exuviae sacrae Constantinopolitanae*, II (Paris: Ernest Leroux, 1904), 176.

26 Eusebius of Caesarea, *Ecclesiastical History*, Books 1-5, trans. Roy J. Deferrari (Washington: Catholic University of America Press, 1953), 78.

27 Wilson, *The Shroud of Turin: Burial Cloth of Jesus?* (New York: Doubleday, 1978), Chapter XIV: "Were Shroud and Mandylion One And The Same Thing?".

28 Fr. Heinrich Pfeiffer, SJ has posited a connection between the Camuliana image and that of the Roman Veronica and Veil of Manoppello. See *The concept of "acheiropoietos", the iconography of the face of Christ and the veil of Manoppello. Proceedings of the International Workshop on the Scientific approach to the Acheiropoietos Images*, ENEA Frascati, Italy, 4-6 May 2010.

29 Hans J.W. Drejvers, "The Image of Edessa in the Syriac Tradition" in *The Holy Face and the Paradox of Representation*, ed. Herbert Kessler and Gerhard Wolf (Bologna: Nuova Alfa, 1998). The True Cross was by far the predominant relic of the crusade period.

30 See Averil Cameron, "The History of the Image of Edessa: The Telling of a Story" in *Harvard Ukrainian Studies*, Vol. 7 (1983), 80-94.

from Jesus to Abgar, which then becomes supplanted by an image of Jesus to Abgar.

COPY OF A LETTER WRITTEN BY ABGAR THE TOPARCH TO JESUS, SENT TO HIM AT JERUSALEM BY THE COURIER ANANIAS

Abgar Uchama, the Toparch, to Jesus the excellent Savior who has appeared in the region of Jerusalem, greeting.

I have heard about you and the cures you accomplish without drugs or herbs. Word has it that you make the blind see and the lame walk, that you heal lepers and cast out unclean spirits and demons, and that you cure those tortured by chronic disease and raise the dead. When I heard all these things about you, I decided that one of two things is true: either you are God and came down from heaven to do these things or you are God's Son for doing them. For this reason I am writing to beg you to take the trouble to come to me and heal my suffering. I have also heard that the Jews are murmuring against you and plot to harm you. Now, my city-state is very small but highly regarded and adequate for both of us.

(He wrote this letter when the divine light had only begun to shine on him. It is appropriate to hear also the letter that Jesus sent him by the same letter carrier. It is only a few lines long but very powerful:)

THE REPLY OF JESUS TO THE TOPARCH ABGAR BY THE COURIER ANANIAS

Blessed are you who believed in me without seeing me! For it is written that those who have seen me will not believe in me and that those who have not seen me will believe and live. Now regarding your request that I come to you, I must first complete all that I was sent to do here, and, once that is completed, must be taken up to the One who sent me. When I have been taken up, I will send one of my disciples to heal your suffering and bring life to you and yours.[31]

In a Syriac version of the tale, *The Doctrine of Addai*, Abgar became privy to the tales of miracles performed by Jesus by an aide who witnessed them first hand, Ananias. Ananias then returned to Judea with Abgar's letter and began to draw a portrait of Jesus. After replying to Abgar with his own letter, Jesus washed his face and dried it on a towel, the result of which – "in some divine and inexpressible manner"[32] – was an

---

31 Eusebius, 1.13. This translated sequence derived from Paul L. Maier, *Eusebius: The Church History, A New Translation with Commentary* (Grand Rapids: Kregel, 1999), 47-50.
32 Herbert L. Kessler, *Spiritual Seeing: Picturing God's Invisibility in Medieval Art* (Philadelphia: Univer-

imprint of Jesus's face. Jesus promised the relic would offer much protection and grace for the people of Edessa. Not only did the cloth cure Abgar upon the king laying eyes on the imprinted face of Jesus, but Abgar was soon baptized, his action thus converting the whole of Edessa to Christianity. And thus a miraculous image of Christ was responsible for the conversion of an Arab country.

Piece from St. Catherine's Monastery in Sinai shows in upper right panel King Abgar receiving portrait of Jesus from Thaddeus, 10th c.

The story of this image of Edessa is one where Jesus is still alive; the Shroud, of course, emphasizes the dead Christ. The very definition of the mandylion evokes a small napkin or handkerchief – the Holy Face – while the Shroud's identity is synonymous with the full body. Ian Wilson suggested that the image of Edessa was in fact the Shroud of Turin folded four times and kept that way, folded like a towel, encased within a protective tile for hundreds of years.[33] When the Shroud was finally displayed in 14th century France, according to this proposal, the mandylion/Shroud was at last exposed in full.

Whatever its true origins, what did the mandylion image look like? Averil Cameron, Oxford professor of Byzantine and Late Antiquity history provided a clue in her citation of Michael the Syrian, a Monophysite (one who believed in Christ only having one nature, his divine nature) and patriarch of the Syriac Orthodox Church until 1199 who spoke of copies made from the original. Cameron noted, "[T]he artist carefully used dim colours *so that the copy would look old.*"[34]

In this way, the mandylion's appearance mirrors that of the Veronica, copies of which barely show a discernible face. In the case of St. Peter's Basilica's own copy, details of the image cannot even be made out. Each year, two basilica canons emerge onto loggia of the St. Veronica pillar to bless the gathered below with the framed image, a ceremony still carried out annually. Other than that brief, distant view, no outsider can access the Veronica chapel to glimpse the image.[35] The indistinct nature of the actual image underscores the variety in Christ's expression seen in Holy Face copies, and may help explain the differences in such copies: some show a luminous face, as in the instance of Dante's description of the Roman Veronica, others depict the face of the suffering Lord amid the Passion, as if detailing the plight in unremitting closeup.

Additionally, to take Michael the Syrian's observation of artist's purposefully aging an image to seem older than it was a step further, these formless Veronicas also echo the sudarium of Oviedo's shapeless bloodstains, and beyond – in this light, the ghostly visage of the Shroud body falls in line with this theme as well. Pope Urban IV, when sending the Holy Face of Laon icon to his sister, abbess at Montreuil-les-dames, commented that the darkness of the image, "the color of Christ's face is the result of his tribulations during his Passion, and of his peregrinations in the sun."[36]

33 Ian Wilson, *Holy Faces, Secret Places: An Amazing Quest for the Face of Jesus* (New York: Doubleday, 1991), 130-144, sp. 142.
34 Cameron, 87. Emphasis mine.
35 See Paul Badde, *The Face of God: The Rediscovery of the True Face of Jesus* (San Francisco: Ignatius Press, 2010), 280-285.
36 Raffaella Zardoni, et al., "The Iconography of the Roman Veronica" in *The European Fortune of the Roman Veronica in the Middle Ages*, 299.

Left, a mandylion copy currently held in the Vatican's Redemptoris Mater chapel; center, the Holy Face of Genoa gifted by Byzantine emperor John V Palaiologos in the 14th c.; right, St. Peter's Veronica image exhibited annually in the basilica

The Veil of Manoppello, housed in the Church of the Holy Face in the Abruzzis, saw a seismic increase in popularity since Pope Benedict XVI's private pilgrimage to the shrine in September 2006. Paul Badde has argued the image is the true veil of Veronica which disappeared around the time of the sack of Rome in 1527. For our purposes, it is necessary to point out a detail about the Manoppello image that is distinct from the Veronica image in St. Peter's: the image, installed in a monstrance-like casing above the church tabernacle, can be visible from both front and back, in the same way a host is seen in a monstrance. Badde examined two panes of broken glass in the Vatican treasury, dated c. 1350, which he believed contained the Manoppello image during its time in Rome. And like the cloth depicted showing Pope Innocent III with the Veronica, the Manoppello image is one where Christ's eyes are opened.

What this also reveals is the practice of donations from pilgrims to various shrines, in particular the Roman Veronica, as well as the growing practice of image copying, much like the architectural copying of the original Holy Sepulchre. As an example of gift-giving, "Three Venetian noblemen visiting Rome for the Jubilee of 1350 offered to the Holy Face a highly accomplished carved frame, decorated with gilded silver and rock crystal."[37] As for copying, "This is attested around 1350 at least in the case of the Veronica, whose copies on cloth or paper were produced and sold in the courtyard of St Peter's by the 'pictores Veronicarum.'"[38] The Holy Face

37 Claudia Bolgia, "Icons 'in the Air': New Settings for the Sacred in Medieval Rome" in *Architecture and Pilgrimage, 1000-1500*, ed. Paul Davies et al. (London: Routledge, 2013), 132.
38 Ibid. See also Jonathan Sumption, *The Age of Pilgrimage: The Medieval Journey to God*, 2003, 260.

of Jaén, dated to c. 1376, is such an example. Indeed, by the time of the institution of the feast of Corpus Christi in 1264, images of the Holy Face of Christ widely proliferated, particularly in England, due in part to the Veronica representations by the monk and chronicler Matthew Paris.[39]

The notion of double-sided imagery suggests that in viewing the Veronica on either side a theme of duality emerges, just as the Shroud shows the frontal and dorsal images of the crucified Christ. Here the connection with an exposed consecrated host is not accidental. That the position of the Manoppello icon is situated above the tabernacle connects the face of Christ with the Eucharistic Lord.[40] The full body image of the Shroud, which could be seen both front and back depending on its fold, goes even further: the body of Christ on the Shroud represents the host transubstantiated into the body of Christ. Taking the theme one step further, Christ Himself embodies dual natures: a completely divine nature and a completely human one, and realized at the Annunciation – the namesake for Geoffroi de Charny's Lirey church.

And to truly correlate the image of the Holy Face with that of the Eucharist, imprints of the face of Christ were impressed on communion hosts. Aden Kumler from the University of Chicago noted, "Although the Holy Face is a rarity among the motifs impressed upon communion wafers by medieval host presses, at least two extant medieval host presses reveal that communion wafers could be and occasionally were imprinted with Christ's *vultus* (countenance) in the period."[41] Additionally, Kumler also detailed other uses of Christ's face. Méreaux were "coin-like tokens distributed to clergy assisting in the celebration of the Mass and sometimes also to Mass-goers [which] also took the form of re-impressions of the Holy Face."[42]

Other contemporary references to the Veronica image in the time of Innocent III's procession of 1208 include Pope Celestine III (d. 1198) showing the cloth to King Philip Augustus of France. Celestine commissioned an ornate ciborium for the Veronica around 1197, as chronicled by Roger of Hoveden.[43] Gervasius of Tilbury, writing sometime between 1209-1214, saw that "the Veronica is a true physical picture of the Lord

39 See Nigel Morgan, "'Veronica' Images and the Office of the Holy Face in Thirteenth Century England" in The European Fortune of the Roman Veronica in the Middle Ages Convivium, 2017, 84-98.

40 Claudia Bolgia detailed a list of major Roman icon tabernacles with sources. See Bolgia, 132ff.

41 "*Signatis...vultus tui*: (Re)impressing the Holy Face before and after the European Cult of the Veronica" in *The European Fortune of the Roman Veronica*, 111.

42 Ibid.

43 Roger of Hoveden, *Gesta regis Ricardi, in Rerum Britannicarum Medii Aevi Scriptores*, XLIX, Vol.2, William Stubbs ed., (London 1867), pp.228-229.

represented as an effigy from the chest upwards;[44] and Gerard of Wales, around 1200, noted its rare expositions but one that "retained in it the expression of his image."[45] So popular did the Roman Veronica become that by the fourteenth century Dante alluded to it in Canto XXXI of the *Paradiso*. Marco Polo mentioned it in his *Travels* when speaking about asbestos salamander: "[T]hey have at Rome a napkin of this stuff, which the Grand Khan sent to the Pope to make a wrapper for the Holy Sudarium of Jesus Christ."[46]

Jacopo Grimaldi was a canon of St. Peter's Basilica as it neared completion of its massive reconstruction in the beginning of the seventeenth century. Grimaldi left drawings of the interior of Old St. Peter's, including a rendition of the Celestine III-commissioned ciborium that housed the Veronica icon. Grimaldi also detailed that when the Veronica was exhibited in a rare ostension, it was accompanied by a baldachin. Embroidered on this miniature baldachin was an image of Christ lying horizontally, hands clasped over the other in the death position. Regrettably, neither the baldachin nor the ciborium survives. The John VII Chapel was destroyed in 1606 during the building of new St. Peter's.

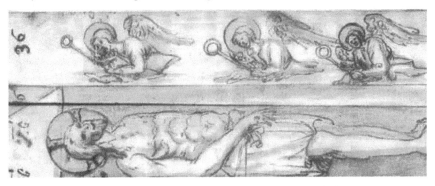

Grimaldi's illustration of supine Christ on miniature baldachin for Roman Veronica

We have already seen how the recumbent position of Christ in the manner as he appears on the Shroud is seen in Easter sepulchral monuments. A similar tradition of venerating the dead Christ emerged in Spain, works called *Crist yacente* (the lying Christ), marked perhaps most notably by the early seventeenth century work, *The Dead Christ of El Pardo* in Madrid by Gregorio Fernández. In general, these depictions of the crucified were quite visceral in the inclusion of blood and twisted nature of Christ's

44 Gervase of Tilbury, *Otia Imperialia: Recreation for an Emperor*, S.E. Banks, J.W. Binns eds and tras., Oxford 2002, book 3, p. 606. Also Dobschütz, *Christusbuilder* 292n14.
45 Gerald of Wales, *Speculum Ecclesiae*, no. 20, 279.
46 *The Travels of Marco Polo*, 1.42

limbs wrought by hours on a cross. However, similar effigies of Christ appeared earlier than these, as contemporaries of the Alsace sepulchres, in the then-Kingdom of Aragon, in Catalonia. At the service of Peter IV of Aragon, two artists of note flourished in the mid-fourteenth century, Aloi de Montbrai and Jaume Cascalls. Their Gothic workshop is credited with executing reclining Christs. While Cascalls today is best remembered for his "Head of Christ," Montbrai was especially noted for his command of depicting accurate anatomy on alabaster.[47]

Often these sculptures served a dual purpose: memorializing Christ while serving as a funereal setting for a tomb, similarly to the Alsacian tombs for bishops. We see an alabaster-chromed, Christ-like sarcophagus crafted by Aloi de Montbrai at the Benedictine monastery of Saint Daniel of Gerona for a tomb with the remains of a martyr, Daniel. This workshop paralleled the Gothic art of André Beauneveu, employed by the Valois dukes, particularly Jean de Berry.

This, then, was the phenomenon of the Holy Face at the time the Shroud emerged in the 14th century.

---

47 Cf. Juan Vicente García Marsilla, *Historia del arte medieval* (Valencia: Universitat de Valencia, 2012), 320.

CHAPTER SIX

THE MAN OF SORROWS

T he *Imago Pietatis* imagery, the Image of Piety, derived from the
Suffering Servant lamentation:

> *He was spurned and avoided by men,*
> *a man of suffering, knowing pain,*
> *Like one from whom you turn your face,*
> *spurned, and we held him in no esteem.*
> *Yet it was our pain that he bore,*
> *our sufferings he endured.*
> *We thought of him as stricken,*
> *struck down by God and afflicted,*
> *But he was pierced for our sins,*
> *crushed for our iniquity.*
> *He bore the punishment that makes us whole,*
> *by his wounds we were healed.*[1]

The Five Wounds of Christ, in reference to the nail wounds in
the feet, hands, and lance wound to the side of the chest – areas of
prominent visibility on the Shroud – developed out of this devotion.
The Man of Sorrows paralleled the eastern Christian cult known,
in Greek, as *Akra Tapeinosis* ("Utmost Humiliation"), or its liturgical usage, *Epitáphios Thrēnos* ("Lamentation upon the Grave").[2] The
oldest known Akra Tapeinosis painting is currently retained in the
Byzantine Museum in Kastoria, Greece. It shows the upper chest and
head of a reposed Christ. His head is tilted towards his right shoulder, almost resting on it, the typical depiction of the final position of
Christ's head in death on the cross. A Eucharistic halo surrounds the
head. Above it, the cross, labeled in Greek, "King of Glory." Below
the cross is the Christogram, the initials for the Greek name of Jesus
Christ, seen on mosaics in church naves wherever there is the Christ
Pantocrator (Deeis): ΙΣ ΧΣ.

---

1 Is 53: 3-5.
2 See Hans Belting, "An Image and Its Function in the Liturgy: The Man of Sorrows in Byzantium"
   in *Dumbarton Oaks Papers*, Vol. 34/35, 1980/81, 1-16.

Hans Belting suggested that the image is something of a paradox: Christ here is dead, but the visible cross and King of Glory title place the setting of the image in the hours between the Crucifixion and the Resurrection, a time that the Catholic Creed asserts was Christ's descent, or harrowing, into hell.[3]

Here we must pause briefly on this matter of the Creed. The harrowing of hell will be covered in the chapter "The Divine Light," but illustrating the articles of the Creed for mortally wounded crusader knights was taken up by Jean de Joinville during the Seventh Crusade while in Acre from 1250-1251. "The purpose of this 'commentary' on the 12 articles of the Creed was to make it impossible for Satan to take possession of the soul of a dying man in his final hours. This was achieved by reading the Credo aloud to him and showing him the illustrations."[4] Joinville, who later reworked the codex at his Champagne estate in 1287, produced a work of art guiding those towards contemplation of their own suffering in union with Christ, something his descendants would accomplish with the exhibition of the Shroud.

The Man of Sorrows cult took off in western Christendom with the emergence of the *Imago Pietatis* icon at Rome's Church of the Santa Croce in Gerusalemme, named as such because soil was brought from Jerusalem at the church's founding. It was originally constructed, according to its origin story, to house Passion relics brought back from the Holy Land to Rome by Constantine's mother, Saint Helena, in 325. The Imago Pietatis has its own competing origin stories for how it appeared in Italy when it did. Gertrud Schiller believed it was the prototype for the Man of Sorrows devotion in the west beginning in the 1200s. Hans Belting postulated it was brought from Constantinople only in the late fourteenth century. A third story is perhaps the most synonymous with its iconography: Pope Saint Gregory the Great (590-604), the pope who helped end a plague endemic in Rome by witnessing a vision of Saint Michael the Archangel, encountered another vision saying Mass: A person attending Pope Gregory's Mass doubted the consecration. Aware of this doubter, Pope Gregory prayed for some kind of sign to convert the unbeliever. The pope's prayer is answered by a vision of Christ's body appearing on the altar at the time of consecration, in the same manner as the Man of Sorrows.

---

3   *Byzantium: Faith and Power*, 222.
4   Jaroslav Folda, *Crusader Art in the Holy Land: From the Third Crusade to the Fall of Acre, 1187-1291* (Cambridge: Cambridge UP, 2005), 500, quoting Robert Scheller, Exemplum.

Imago pietatis (Man of Sorrows) in the Basilica di Santa Croce in Gerusalemme, Rome c. 1300

In relief, the half figure of Christ emerges from the sepulcher as the Man of Sorrows, lunette late 14th c. Two papal coat of arms flank the Imago Pietatis, not unlike the coat of arms on the Lirey badge and mould (MuseiD-Italia)

Israhel van Meckenem's engraving from the 1490s of the Mass of St. Gregory, a work of art packed with Passion imagery. Note the Veronica above the patibulum-shaped cross

The Man of Sorrows motifs conflate Eucharistic imagery with sepulcher imagery. This dominant genre of medieval art falls under the German
term *andachtsbilder,* in which the imago pietatis, the Pieta, graphic Crucifixion scenes, mournful entombments and others constitute imagery
designed to spawn affective piety and private devotion.

* * *

Two Passion works at the Cleveland Museum of Art reveal the emo-
tional range of the andachtsbilder.

"Christ and Saint John the Evangelist," c. 1300-1320 from the Swabia
region outside Stuttgart west of Strasbourg, is a tender, simple sculpture
visualizing John 13:23. The museum notes, "Many of these devotional
sculptures adorned the chapels of Dominican convents," and that "this
sculpture reflects the fundamental religious beliefs rooted in the mysticism that dominated the period."[5] "Calvary with a Carthusian monk," c.
1389-1395, is attributed to Jean de Beaumetz, official court painter to
Philip the Bold, duke of Burgundy. The sufferings endured by Christ are
not left to the imagination here, as the museum's notes indicate:

> The Carthusians were intensely devoted to the Passion of Christ; par-
> ticularly bloody images of the Crucifixion often decorated their cells.
> Isolated from one another, the monks contemplated the sacrifice of
> Christ (emphasized here by the presence of a Carthusian monk at
> the foot of the cross) creating an empathetic connection with the
> suffering of the Virgin who faints in the arms of the two Marys. Saint
> John the Evangelist, on the right, bows his head in sorrow.[6]

Christ and Saint John the Evangelist (left); (right), Calvary with a Carthusian monk

5 https://www.clevelandart.org/art/1928.753
6 https://www.clevelandart.org/art/1964.454

Most depictions of the Man of Sorrows isolate Christ from other characters – Christ and Christ alone must endure the trials of the Passion. Similarly, it is only the crucifix that hangs in the sanctuary – mourners, the crowd, guards, the good thief and bad thief, all those depicted on the *via dolorosa* have disappeared. Or, rather, they are enmeshed into the congregation. From the pews in a church nave, the faithful gaze towards the sanctuary as if at the foot of the cross on Calvary.

Late medieval church architecture honed this concept with the *jube,* a screen that ran the length of the chancel.[7] A rood loft, a crucifix with typically the Blessed Mother and Saint John on each side, was surmounted atop the center of the screen. This separation from the high altar and the nave was meant to enhance reverence and solemnity of the consecrated host in the Tabernacle. All but a few churches in the Latin west today contain such an architectural element. The post-Vatican II church viewed such separation as an obstacle to the communal gathering around the Lord's table.[8] In the Christian East, a similar partition separates the Holy of Holies from everything else. It is the *iconostasis*, the wall or screen often composed of icons and holy imagery with two central doors – the "Beautiful Gates" – that bridge the ensuing ritual within the sanctuary, the Eucharist, with the faithful in the nave. These doors have also been referred to as holy doors, mostly in the west, and royal doors, named as such to mark the entrance of the Byzantine emperor. Ceremonial Holy Doors are still present in Catholic basilicas and cathedrals, now situated in the narthex, the entrance of the church proper. Iconostases are an integral part in the Divine Liturgy, as their purpose is not merely decorative, but themselves contributing to the presence of Christ.

Consider, for instance, Bright Week, known in the Latin west as Easter Week. The Beautiful Gates are flung open, and stay that way for this glorious week. He is Risen, the common Easter phrase, here is visually symbolized: the gates, like the stone covering the tomb, are open. The doors, normally always closed, indeed the whole of the iconostasis, are like a portal into a most hallowed area, where Christ is manifested. It is no coincidence that the Holy of Holies, the sanctuary, was derived from the layout of the Temple in Jerusalem, the one pulverized by the Romans in AD 70. The faithful had just participated in the most wrenching week of the year, that of Christ's passion. But the tomb was empty. Joy, not sorrow, reigned. And through the open doors in this week the faithful could

---

7 Steven J. Schloeder, *Architecture in Communion* (San Francisco: Ignatius Press, 1998), 78.
8 Ibid., 76.

glimpse a stirring sight: on the altar table, the site of the Holy Sacrifice, rests a cloth – the *epitaphios threnos*, the Lamentation Upon the Grave.

Rood screen with St. John and the Blessed Mother flanking the crucified Christ | cdttarn, cc-by-2.0

Iconostasis in Hagia Triada Greek Orthodox Church, Istanbul | Dosseman, Creative Commons Attribution-Share Alike 4.0 International

Example of epitaphios threnos cloth with crown of thorns around cross | ΙΣΧΣΝΙΚΑ-888
https://creativecommons.org/licenses/by-sa/4.0/deed.en

Inspired by not only the Great Aër, the large veil covering the chalice and paten in the Divine Liturgy, but also the *katapetasma*, the curtains in the Temple of Jerusalem, "the oldest surviving epitaphios dates to the end of the thirteenth century"[9] and resembling the *antimension*, the silk or linen cloth on which the Eucharist is celebrated, the significance of epitaphios in Divine Liturgy placed upon the Holy Table links not only the altar with the tomb, but the entire space beyond the iconostasis. The Epitaphios is ceremoniously brought onto the table during the entombment portion of the Great Friday liturgy, where it remains into Great Saturday. When placing the bread and wine on the altar during the Great Friday liturgy, the priest says, "Taking your most pure body from the rood, the pious Joseph wrapped it in a shroud with ointments and placed it into a new grave."[10] During Matins on Saturday, the icon is processed around the church interior as if on a bier, cloth exposed for the faithful to venerate as it passes, replete with candles and incense.

---

9 *Byzantium: Faith and Power (1261-1557)*, ed. Helen C. Evans (New York: MetPublications, 2004), 187A., 312.
10 Eugene Csocsan de Varallja, "The Turin Shroud and Hungary" (1987), 14n65.

Symeon of Thessaloniki describes the procession: "After it come the deacons one after another who have the order of the angels; then those carrying the divine gifts; and after them all the others and those carrying over their head the sacred great veil which has the depiction of Jesus naked and dead."[11] Roland Betancourt observed mosaics from the Monastery of the Great Lavra, the first monastery on Mount Athos, where "various angel-deacons process in the Great Entrance of the Celestial Liturgy, carrying liturgical implements, while across their backs and shoulders and help by strings to the hands are various examples of midsized aëres."[12]

(Top) Angel-Deacons in Celestial Liturgy while carrying the Great Aër over head, wall painting, Holy Monastery of Grachanica, Serbia, c. 1320 | (Below) Commemorative medal of Louis I, Duke of Savoy, 1453, with Shroud over head

11 Steven Hawkes-Teeples, *Symeon of Thessalonika: The Liturgical Commentaries* (Toronto 2011), 126-127.

12 Conrad Betancourt, "The Thessaloniki Epitaphios: Notes on Use and Context" in *Greek, Roman, and Byzantine Studies* 55 (2015), 489–535.

Shroud researchers have often found in epitaphios such as that of Stefan Uroš II Milutin imagery "so strikingly reminiscent of the Shroud's front-of-body image that, whether directly or indirectly, it can hardly be other than that image's progeny or precursor."[13] Epitaphoi commemorated individuals of stature, deceased or otherwise, such as the Epitaphios of the Emperor John Cantacuzenus (reigned 1347-1354, d. 1383), who lived out his days as a monk on Mount Athos. The epitaphios of King Stefan Uroš II Milutin, King of Serbia (reigned 1282-1321), son of King Stefan I and Helen of Anjou, contains a Slavonic inscription: "Remember, O God, the soul of your servant Milutin Uroš." A late fourteenth century Byzantine epitaphios from the Transfiguration Monastery in central Greece inscribes the following:

> I believe in your great Second Coming, oh King, and I longingly anticipate, I am astonished, and quiver how will I look at you, oh Judge; how will I tell you my deeds; who will I use as a mediator; how will I escape hell; I renounce myself; I turn to you now. Save me, oh Savior, with the gift of your compassion, through your mercy.[14]

The corresponding imagery around the recumbent Christ – angels, a six-winged seraphim, interlocked rings and countless stars – take the viewer beyond the physical tomb in Jerusalem to a celestial, numinous perspective, reminding one of Charlemagne's chapel dome with 144 stars. Indeed, "Its style is ascetic and extremely symbolic, since its meaning is eucharistic-liturgical, even eschatological, pointing to the immediate and also the coming era."[15]

Epitaphios of Serbian king Stefan Uroš II Milutin (d. 1321)

13 Ian Wilson, *The Blood and the Shroud,* (New York: Doubleday 1998), 137.
14 *Byzantium: Faith and Power*, 187B, 313-314.
15 Ibid., 313.

90

CHAPTER SEVEN

THE SHROUD AND THE GRAIL

The Holy Grail – long the favorite subject for conspiracy theories.[1] Attempts have also been made to identify it as if not the Shroud then its reliquary casket.[2] But in just a cursory glance into the deep depths of Arthurian lore, we can see how the quest for the Holy Grail is fulfilled not so much in the artifact of the Shroud, but in what it represents: the body and blood of the Lamb of God.

Although Pope Urban IV decreed the Feast of Corpus Christi in 1264, it was slow to gain traction throughout Christendom. Urban's own devotion to both the corporal and Eucharistic body of the Lord is evidenced in the popular, if unconfirmed, story of his coming into possession of what is known today as the Holy Face of Laon, after Urban (then still Archdeacon Pantaleon of Laon Cathedral), sent the icon to his sister, Abbess Sibylle at Montreuil-les-Dames, in July 1249. The inscription is in late first millennium Slavonic, just as the words on the epitaphios of King Stefan Uroš II Milutin, that says *Obraz Gospodin na Ubruzje*: "the image of the Lord on the sudarium-shroud."[3] Pantaleon is said to have urged his sister in his accompanying letter to look upon it "like the holy Veronica, as its true image and likeness."[4] As he was Innocent IV's papal legate to Prussia and Polonia in the 1240s, Shroud enthusiasts have attempted to connect the production of the icon with the Benedictine monastery at Szavaszentdemeter in the Srem district of modern Serbia, where a few Shroud enthusiasts suggested the Shroud was kept in the years after the sack of Constantinople.[5]

In any case, for the one who will establish the Feast of Corpus Christi – and a native of Troyes at that – Pope Urban IV, the Holy Face of Laon icon

---

1   For starters, Baigent, Leigh, Lincoln, *The Holy Blood, The Holy Grail* (London: Jonathan Cape, 1982).

2   Noel Currer-Briggs, *The Holy Grail and the Shroud of Christ* (London: ARA Publications, 1984) and *The Shroud and the Grail* (London: Weidenfeld & Nicolson, 1987); Wilson, *The Blood and the Shroud* (New York: Doubleday, 1998), sp. 169-171; Daniel C. Scavone, "Joseph of Arimathea, the Holy Grail and the Edessa Icon" in Arthuriana (Winter 1999), 3-31.

3   Andre Grabar, *La Sainte-Face de Laon : le Mandylion dans l'art orthodoxe* (Prague: Seminarium Kondakovianum, 1931). Also Jannic Durand, ed. *Byzance: L'art Byzantin Dans Les Collections Publicques Francaises* (Paris, 1992), 475.

4   Cf. Jean-Michel Spieser, Elisabeth Yota, "Mandylion" in *Sainte Face de Laon, in Il volto di Cristo*, op. Cit., 97.

5   de Varallja, 21.

united the mandylion traditions of the East with the Roman Veronica cult in the west.

The Holy Face of Laon

Currer-Briggs, who in his book *The Holy Grail and the Shroud of Christ*, subscribed to the hypothesis that the mandylion and Shroud of Turin are one in the same. He connects the Holy Face of Laon to a badly preserved mandylion fresco in Serbia's Gradac Monastery, built between 1277-1282 by the queen consort of Serbia, Helen of Anjou, mother of King Stefan Uroš II Milutin. Currer-Briggs specifically points out the similar trellis or lattice shapes on that mosaic as also visible on the Laon icon. "The term lattice or trellis is synonymous with grid or grill, and they all derive from the medieval French word 'greil' or 'greille.'"[6] For Currer-Briggs, this was evidence of a decorative grill behind which was the Shroud, folded in such a way as to only reveal the face.[7]

---

6 Noel Currer-Briggs, *The Holy Grail and the Shroud of Christ*, 23.
7 Ibid.

Mandylion fresco in Gradac Monastery, Serbia | The Svetlana Tomeković Database of Byzantine Art, Princeton University

Rather, we can see in broader cultural movements in the centuries leading up to Geoffroi de Charny and the twilight of the Middle Ages the culmination of the Grail quest in the Holy Eucharist. Indeed, the letter of affirmation from Bishop Henri de Troyes to Geoffroi de Charny on his faith and his success in establishing a "divine cult" at Notre-Dame de Lirey is dated Saturday, May 28, 1356 – a date which corresponds with the octave of Corpus Christi for that year.

Troyes, the residency of the counts of Champagne, was instrumental in disseminating Grail stories throughout Champagne and Burgundy, particularly in the work of Chretien de Troyes (d. 1191). Chretien was the poet-in-residence at the court of Marie, daughter of Eleanor of Aquitaine and her first husband, King Louis VII of France, and her husband Henri, count of Champagne. Eleanor's influence as queen consort of England – after her annullment from Louis VII – captivated the populace, from common people to poets.

The newfound realm of the House of Plantagenet under the rule of Henry II and Eleanor planted seeds for the future Hundred Years' War between England and France. A popular literary work at this time embraced by Henry II's court and which generated much influence across Christendom was Geoffrey of Monmouth's *The History of the Kings of Britain*, a pseudo-historical rip-roaring jaunt through British history that blended fact and fiction to great acclaim. A Homeric, Celtic response to the Frankish *chanson de geste* (heroic deeds) of Charlemagne, the opus fell under the common genre known as the Matter of Britain. Of particular interest was its inclusion of a British king named Uther Pendragon and his son, the once and future king, Arthur. Other characters included in Monmouth's work were a magician called Merlin and other kings named Lear and Cymbeline.

J. Douglas Bruce, in *The Evolution of Arthurian Romance*, critiqued: "The conception of Arthur as a great medieval monarch, the ideal representative of chivalry – not a merely fairy-tale king – originated, we may say, entirely with Geoffrey of Monmouth."[8] Monmouth depicts a wounded Arthur, after battle against Mordred, promising to return in glory:

> I will give thee here my kingdom, and defend thou my Britons ever in thy life, and maintain them all the laws that have stood in my days, and all the good laws that in Uther's days stood. And I will fare thee to Avalun, to the fairest of all maidens, to Argante the queen, an elf most fair, and she shall make my wounds all sound, make me all whole with healing draughts. And afterwards I will come again to my kingdom and dwell among the Britons with great joy.[9]

The *History of the Kings of Britain*, written in Latin, was soon translated into French as *Roman de Brut* by Robert Wace. It is Wace who adds new Arthurian motifs such as the Round Table. Bruce noted, "[Wace] accordingly contributed largely to the spread of interest in the Arthurian stories, for in the Middle Ages, as well as now, more people could enjoy a tale in the vernacular than in Latin."[10] Of those was the court of Henry and Eleanor, to whom Wace personally presented a copy of *Roman de Brut*, and who became chief proponents of spreading the work across their Angevin empire. It eventually reached the court of Eleanor's daughter in Champagne, Marie, and her husband, Henri I, where it would have tremendous influence on their poet-in-residence, Chretien de Troyes.

Chretien's Arthurian cycle, *Eric and Enide* (1170), *Cliges* (1170), *Lancelot* (1172), *Yvain* (1173) were produced under the patronage of Henri and Marie, with the exception of the incomplete *Perceval, the Story of the Grail* (1175). That was commissioned by Philip of Alsace, count of Flanders, who yearned for success in the Holy Land and eventually perished

---

8   J. Douglas Bruce, *The evolution of Arthurian romance from the beginnings down to the year 1300* (Gloucester: Peter Smith, 1958), 20.
9   Ibid., 33.
10 Ibid.

at the Siege of Acre in 1191 (and is buried at Clairvaux Abbey). Though Chretien did not invent the Arthurian legends, he singularly influenced later efforts, namely by extending the Arthurian universe beyond Arthur himself. With the embellishment of side characters and plots, Arthur's knights became the leading men of their own poems, such as Lancelot and Perceval. In this way, Chretien deepened the notion of knights and quests, adding a crucial, original motif that would forever be associated with the Knights of the Round Table: the Grail.

Additionally, perhaps governed both by his grasp of Classical literature (Ovid, for one) and by the affecting presence of Marie and her mother, Eleanor, Chretien strengthened the importance of the feminine in his cycle, fleshing out characters' desires and motivations beyond the otherwise simplified damsel in distress or complacent queen. J. Douglas Bruce:

> The difference between the ideals of the society of such a court as Marie's in the second half of the twelfth century and those of the earlier time represented by the chansons de geste is connected, above all, with the improved position of women. This accords with the general advance of civilization from the unrestricted reign of physical force in the earlier Middle Ages and is manifest even in the political arrangements of the time, since women were now permitted to inherit the great fiefs. The centre from which this movement radiated was the south of France--the land of Eleanor of Poitiers (Aquitaine) and the land where all ideas of social and intellectual liberty had so far received their highest development.[11]

Now in Chretien's version, the enduring elements found in *Perceval* took on heightened relevancy for his audiences in the wake of the crusades. For instance, the young knight, Perceval, discovers the guardian of the Grail, the Fisher King, when he is, appropriately, fishing, but wounded and alone, unable to heal. In Chretien's time of scribing *Perceval*, Amalric I, king of Jerusalem, died of dysentery, consistently besieged by Nur ad-Din, Saladin, the new Sultan of Egypt, and covert attacks by the Hashshashin, the Islamic Order of Assassins. Twenty years later, the Hashshashin assassinated the king-elect of Jerusalem, Conrad de Montferrat, older brother of Boniface, in Acre in a garden portico where he died by stab wounds, leaving behind a pregnant wife, Isabella. The man who emerged as the husband to the new Queen of Jerusalem, Isabella, was none other than the son of Henri, Count of Champagne, veteran of the Second Crusade and patron of Chretien de Troyes, and Marie of France – Henri II.

---

11 Ibid., 105

Amalric's successor was his son, himself a wounded king – the leper king Baldwin IV, whose short, ineffectual reign focused on placating Saladin's advances on Jerusalem had enormous consequences for the unstable future of the Latin kingdom. Baldwin's cousin happened to be Philip, Count of Flanders and commissioner of Chretien's *Perceval*.

On another level, the Fisher King also was recognized as the King of Kings. "Follow me, and I will make you fishers of men."[12] Later, the one who multiplied the loaves and fishes will be wounded on the Cross by a lance into the side, under the sign of Pilate: *This is the king of the Jews.* The Vicar of Christ, the pope, the successor to St. Peter as the bishop of Rome, wears the fisherman's ring. In the early Christian community, when the faith was underground in the catacombs, the symbol for Christ the Savior was a fish.

Perceval then enters the otherworldly realm of the Grail Castle where he witnesses an unusual ritual: in the presence of the wounded king, groaning on his litter, a procession unfolds featuring a bleeding white lance, blood dripping from the tip, two multi-branched candelabra with lighted candles, and a woman carrying a gold "graal," an ambiguous vessel nonetheless life giving in some way – and bursting with light. Another woman completes the procession with a silver platter before the elements are arranged on an altar-like table in preparation for either a meal, or something more. Robert A. Johnson has defined this moment as the "Grail Hunger," when the immature and Godless seek elsewhere what can only be found in the contents of the Grail offers. "The hunger for 'something,' the Saturday night restlessness, the tires squealing around the corner are all not-so-distant echoes of the Grail-castle hunger."[13] In Grail terms, the immature and Godless reside in the "waste land," which T.S. Eliot invoked in his poem of the same name.

Emma Jung has connected the woman bearing the graal as a mediatrix into the unconsciousness, not unlike the understanding of the Virgin Mary as mediatrix of all graces.[14] Perceval, however, while in his knightly training to join Arthur's court is admonished by his mentor to keep quiet, fails to ask clarifying questions on what he observes, including the all important question, "To whom does the Grail serve?"

Chretien blended the saga's pagan roots with a new narrative thrust, one that served the foundation for the "Grail hunger" that rumbled in

---

12 Mt 4:19

13 Robert A. Johnson, *He: Understanding Male Psychology* (New York: Harper & Row, 1989), 54.

14 Emma Jung and Marie-Louise von Franz, *The Grail Legend* (New York: CJ Jung Foundation, 1970), 65.

every succeeding generation. It is important to note Chretien does not associate the grail as anything beyond some kind of vessel. That *Perceval* was left unfinished only added to the seismic impact it immediately struck those traveling to and fro from Outremer, leaving rapt audiences in a cliff-hanger state.

Even a Cistercian monk contributed a version, *Queste del seint graal* (c. 1220). Miri Rubin noted, "The *Queste* ... created a quest which was a route towards self-discovery, in search for an ultimate reward. The terms in which both the route and the reward were described are couched with eucharistic meanings and associations, the grail being both symbol and object, like the very eucharist, symbol and essence, even though it is never quite pinned down to one meaning being at once chalice, lamb, ciborium, and the Supper's tray."[15]

But it was another troubadour, Robert de Boron, who interwove a Christian presence so effectively within the Arthurian romances that it was only after Boron did the Holy Grail forever become associated with the cup, or chalice, from the Last Supper. It is not clear whether Robert de Boron traveled with his crusading patron, Gauthier de Montbeliard – a colorful character in his own right – on his exploits with fellow men-at-arms Robert de Joinville, uncle of Jean de Joinville, and Gauthier III de Brienne, the hero of St. Francis of Assisi's younger days.[16]

Gauthier de Montebeliard married the daughter of the king of Jerusalem and became Regent of the kingdom of Cyprus. Prior to the arrival of Latin Catholics after Saladin's capture of Jerusalem, Cyprus remained loyal to the Byzantine Court and the Orthodox Church, with the island home to some 15 bishops. The religious center of Cyprus was anchored by the Bishop of Lambousa on the north coast of the island, near Kyrenia. The headquarters of the Bishop of Lambousa was a venerable monastery originally built on the ruins of a sixth century Christian basilica. The name of the monastery, though dedicated to the Virgin Mary, is better known for its colloquial name – Acheiropoietos Monastery. A 1918 description of historic monuments in Cyprus indicated the monastery's name, Acheiropoietos, derived from a local tradition that the Shroud spent some time at this very monastery.[17]

---

15 Miri Rubin, *Corpus Christi: The Eucharist in Late Medieval Culture* (Cambridge: Cambridge UP, 1991), 140. For an extended discussion on Grail imagery and the Eucharist, 139-142.

16 Villehardouin, 9.

17 Dr. Alessandro Camiz, Assoc. Prof. on the faculty of Architecture and Design of Özyeğin University, Istanbul, advised there is no historical record of an icon, except the building's name, and thus an immaterial historical source. Correspondence with author, Nov. 30, 2018.

St. Francis of Assisi venerates the Holy Face | Courtesy Paul Badde

Boron is credited as the author of a Grail cycle that comprises three titles: *Perceval, Merlin,* and the first entry in Boron's trilogy, *Joseph of Arimathea,* a wholly original contribution to the Arthurian romances to that time. It is this work that primarily concerns us, a legacy left on future Grail cycles and on the enduring consciousness of the Grail itself.[18]

For as central a role that Joseph of Arimathea plays in the Grail legends as the bearer of the sacred vessel containing Christ's blood, he speaks no words in the four canonical Gospels. Instead, Robert de Boron's *Joseph of Arimathea* is inspired more by the apocryphal *Gospel of Nicodemus* than the four canonical Gospels. The central conflict revolves around Joseph's role as a secret disciple of the crucified Jesus. Jewish authorities imprison Joseph, only to find him somehow escaped, rescued by Jesus:

> Who art thou, Lord? And he said unto me: I am Jesus, whose body thou didst beg of Pilate, and didst clothe me in clean linen and cover my face with a napkin, and lay me in thy new cave and roll a great stone upon the door of the cave. And I said to him that spake with me: Show me the place where I laid thee. And he brought me and showed me the place where I laid him, and the linen cloth lay therein, and the napkin that was upon his face. And I knew that it was Jesus.

18 *Merlin and the Grail: Joseph of Arimathea, Merlin, Perceval: The Trilogy of Arthurian Prose Romances attributed to Robert de Boron,* trans. Nigel Bryant (Woodbridge: Boydell & Brewer, 2001). The following summary of Joseph of Arimathea is derived from Bryant's translation.

St. John looks on as Joseph of Arimathea veils the body of Christ, c. 1429 | Courtesy Paul Badde

Boron's *Joseph of Arimathea* picks up with the events of the Passion, though here Joseph is an associate of Pontius Pilate, a knight in charge of five other knights, and present when Judas negotiated the thirty pieces of silver with Jewish authorities to betray Jesus. After the crucifixion, as in the Gospels, Pilate grants the body to Joseph, and here, Nicodemus. Pilate also hands off a vessel to Joseph, an item associated with the crucified Nazarene.

Upon washing the body, prompting a fresh flow of blood from the wounds of Christ, Joseph utilizes the vessel to catch the Redeemer's blood. As with the *Gospel of Nicodemus*, Boron then details "the Harrowing" – Christ's descent into Hell and subsequent resurrection. Because of the mysterious resurrection event and disappearance of Christ's body, Joseph is thrown into solitary confinement in a Roman prison in Jerusalem. In a vision, Christ gives Joseph the vessel containing his Precious Blood. Here, a direct distinction between the Passion and the centrality of the Mass, the Holy Sacrifice, is linked: in addition to sharing with Joseph the sacred words of consecration, Christ reveals the meaning of the sacred elements to forever be enacted: Christ's flesh and blood become bread and wine; the tomb is the altar; the linen burial cloth becomes the square-sized linen corporal on which the consecrated elements are placed; the vessel containing the blood becomes the chalice; the tombstone becomes the paten, the small plate containing the hosts.

Though Christ hands over the sacred vessel, Joseph remains in prison – for forty years, sustained by the presence of the vessel. The Roman emperor's son, Vespasian, afflicted with leprosy, then enters the narrative seeking healing and is told he can only be healed by something related to Christ. Here, the character Veronica is introduced, specifically associated with her towel on which Christ wiped his face en route to Golgotha. In Boron, Veronica and her veil are brought to Rome, where the relic then cures Vespasian.

Soon, Vespasian travels to Judea, demanding Jesus be brought to him. (In the actual historical timeline that Boron's narrative occurs, the military figure and future emperor Vespasian besieged Jerusalem to the point of destruction in the Great Jewish Revolt.) Vespasian is told only one person can meet Vespasian's demand, and he is brought to the dungeon where Joseph is kept. Vespasian is amazed to find the Arimathean so healthy after forty years in prison, and is so compelled by Joseph's commitment to the faith he converts to Christianity. Though there is no historical account of Vespasian encountering Joseph of Arimathea, there is a curious line in Suetonius's biography of Vespasian in the Roman historian's *Lives of the Twelve Caesars*: "[O]ne of the noble captives, named Joseph, when he was put in chains, kept affirming that he would soon be freed by Vespasian."[19]

Boron then documents Joseph upon his liberation, setting off to evangelize in distant lands along with his sister, Enygeus, and his sister's husband, Hebron (Bron).

---

19 Bruce, 239.

As the story progresses, eponymous images connected to the Last Supper and Passion gradually appear: the Grail table with a fish caught by Bron evokes the Upper Room table and breaking of bread. That Veronica also factors in directly connotes the enduring theme of a wounded king (or emperor) healed by a relic of Christ, particularly one associated with his own body.

Eventually, an angel announces:

> The Lord knows Bron for a worthy man and it was therefore his will that he should go fishing. He is to keep the vessel after Joseph, who must instruct him properly, especially concerning the holy words which God spake to Joseph in the prison, which are sweet and precious, gracious and merciful, and which are properly called the Secrets of the Grail.

Bron then becomes known as "The Rich Fisher." Joseph transfers the vessel into his possession, and it is the descendants of Bron who become the guardians of the Grail, the Fisher Kings.

J. Douglas Bruce notes that in *Joseph of Arimathea* Boron is less interested in the Grail as it pertains to "the marvelous power of supplying food and drink, youth, health, and strength. Such a conception of its power is found in some Grail romances later than his. With Robert, however, it is a vessel of 'grace' in whose service only the good and pure can remain."

Robert de Boron's *Joseph of Arimathea* manages to effectively place this "sacred vessel" at the center of a narrative that weaves a Christian backstory into an Arthurian theme. It effortlessly builds off the recognizable events of the four canonical Gospels but owes as much to apocryphal literature, the role of relics, but above all the centrality of the memorial of Christ's death and resurrection as ritualized in the Mass.

Although there has been much analyses on what "grail" or "graal" mean, both etymologically and physically, Bruce speaks plainly and most effectively on what the Grail represents at the heart of Robert de Boron's *Joseph*:

> The Grail is present with Christ at the Last Supper; like Christ it is brought to Pilate; Joseph of Arimathea receives it, as he receives the body of our Lord; it is present at the entombment, remains then concealed and at last reappears with the risen Christ. It is plain, then, that we have in Robert's history of the Holy Grail a characteristic piece of medieval symbolism. The Grail is the symbol of Christ's body."[20]

---

20 Ibid.

Icon of Joseph of Arimathea, with Shroud and Grail

In Geoffroi de Charny's own life, we see a conflation of Arthurian themes, aside from his family's association with a Grail-like object in the Shroud. Geoffroi was a poet and writer on chivalric themes, like Chretien de Troyes and Robert de Boron before him. By all contemporary accounts he was an esteemed knight of virtue and justice. And he was instrumental in a royal order chronicler Jean Froissart likened to Arthur's Round Table – "the first order of knighthood established by a French king."[21] Its

21 Dominique DeLuca, "Grandes Chroniques de France, c. 1378-79" in *Myth and Mystique: Cleve-*

name was the Company of Our Lady of the Noble House, but it was better known as the Order of the Star.[22]

The order's inaugural feast was set by King Jean II the Good for January 6, 1352, the eve of Epiphany.[23] Richard Barber suggested that "it is possible that [Geoffroi de Charny] had been connected with the plans for this order since Jean II originally proposed it in 1344."[24] Charny was close with the king on a number of campaigns before Jean's ascension to the throne in August 1350 after the death of his father, Philippe VI, when he was known as the duke of Normandy. Barber also notes Charny "wrote one of his works specifically for the order, the *Questions on Jousts, Tournaments and War*."[25]

Some of France's most illustrious knights joined the order's roster that eventually numbered 300. Alongside Geoffroi de Charny were the king's sons: the dauphin, Louis, duke of Anjou; Jean, duke of Berry; Philip, duke of Orleans and future duke of Burgundy; the king's brother Philip, duke of Orleans; Gauthier VI de Brienne, duke of Athens; Pierre, duke of Bourbon, whose father "founded the confraternity of the Holy Sepulcher located on the rue St. Denis in Paris in 1325 to express the living memory of the sacred place in the Holy Land. One of the objectives of this confraternity was to propagate devotion to the tomb of Christ that would in turn reinforce the presence of the pilgrims at the Holy Sepulcher in Jerusalem."[26] Another member, perhaps an honorary one, was Humbert II de Viennois. Formerly the Dauphin of Viennois and leader of Geoffroi de Charny's sole crusade in the 1340s (although it is not entirely clear if de Charny actually was on this Smyrinote crusade),[27] Humbert eventually ceded his lands and possessions to King Philippe VI in 1349[28] and entered the Dominicans. In 1352, Humbert, who died in 1355, offered to the Dominicans of Montfleury a crystal tube that encased a thorn.[29]

---

land's Table Fountain, ed. Stephen N. Fliegel and Elina Gertsman (London: D. Giles Limited), 2016), 147.

22 Jean Froissart, *Chronicles de Froissart*. Ed. Buchon, Paris: Polain, t. II, 173.

23 Leopold Pannier, *La noble-maison de Saint-Ouen, la villa Clippiacum et l'ordre de l'Etoile : d'après les documents originaux* (Paris: A. Franck, 1872), 95.

24 Barber, 370.

25 Ibid.

26 Sadler, 89n.77.

27 Philip Contamine, "Geoffroy de Charny (debut du XIVe siecle-1356)," in *Histoire et societe: Melanges offerts a Georges Duby*, ed. M. Balard, vol. 2 (Aix-en-Provence: Publications de l'Universite de Provence, 1992), 110-111.

28 The official date of the cessation was July 16. See *Art de verifier les dates*, 763.

29 Dor, 27.

14th c. miniature of King John II of France with members of the Order of the Star, including Geoffroi de Charny; the company celebrates a feast, below | Folio 394r, Grandes Chroniques de France de Charles V 1375-80, Bibliothèque Nationale, Paris

Many of those in the order perished or were kidnapped in the decisive loss at Poitiers on September 19, 1356. When King Jean founded the order in 1351, he specified two identification badges for the members: one large badge pinned to a cloak, and a smaller one as a ring. "He ordered that the badges be designed in the form of a white star with a roundel of azure containing a little gold sun in the center. This emblem has been interpreted as a representation of the star of Bethlehem, as well as a symbolic allusion to the Virgin Mary and Christ."[30]

30 DeLuca, 146.

A fourteenth century table fountain – the only intact object of its kind to come down to us – was acquired by the Cleveland Museum of Art in 1924.[31] The automata "naturally fit into the courtly impulse for ostentation, the desire to impress through spectacular ornaments and ceremony."[32] Stephen Fliegel, Cleveland's former medieval art curator, posited the fountain was a possible gift to the Order of the Star, indicative by the very presence of eight shield-shaped escutcheons each with an eight-pointed star. This design is nearly identical with the order's identification badges as depicted in the miniature in *Grandes Chroniques de France*, an illuminated manuscript owned by the dauphin and order member, Charles V.[33]

Left: 14th c. Table Fountain | Cleveland Museum of Art. Right: Close-up of star enamel on Table Fountain suggesting association with Order of the Star | Cleveland Museum of Art

The table fountain's Gothic architecture resembles a variety of masterpieces, from the lower chapel of the Sainte-Chapelle to the translucent enamel of the *Shrine of Thomas Basin* (c. 1320-1340). The fountain's physical beauty was complemented by its sensual ability to scent a room by perfumed water. One can imagine its mechanical movement churning while the king held court with the order, as "each of the companions recount all the adventures, the shameful and the glorious."[34]

While this particular table fountain's practical function was secular (though its style resembles liturgical objects such as monstrance bases

31 See *Myth and Mystique* and https://www.clevelandart.org/art/1924.859.
32 Fliegel, "The Cleveland Table Fountain" in *Myth and Mystique*, 12.
33 Ibid., 46.
34 Fliegel, 49 quoting Jean le Bel in *Chronique de Jean le Bel*, ed. J. Viard, E. Deprez, 4 vols (Paris: Librairies Renouard, 1904), 2:204-206.

and candlestick supports), it here serves as a segue into exploring sublime Christian symbolism. Secondly, it demonstrates the sophisticated (and expensive) penchant for members of the Order of the Star and their kin in not only possessing artistic objects, but as patrons of early Netherlandish painters. That will be the subject of our final expedition into this lost world.

Shrine of Thomas Basin, Paris. C. 1320-1340 | Morgan Library & Museum

Let us begin with the patroness of the Order of the Star, the Blessed Virgin Mary. King Jean is clear in a June 1352 letter to Henri de Culent, who donated his land for the order's church, that the church was named in Our Lady's honor – specifically, Notre-Dame de l'Estelle, Our Lady of the Star.[35] Though the order's first celebration occurred on the eve of Epiphany, the feast celebrating the Three Magi who found the Christ Child by way of the star, Mary is the *Stella Maris*, Star of the Sea. It also evokes, it should be noted, the pilgrim trail of Saint James to Santiago de Compostela, dubbed "the milky way" by travelers able to follow the night stars to guide them.

35 Pannier, 79.

Jan van Eyck, while in the court of Philip the Good, duke of Burgundy (d. 1467), completed his oil painting *Madonna and Child at the Fountain* (1439). The setting is a rose garden. A thin brass fountain with catch basin is in the foreground, to Mary's right. She cradles the Christ Child who snuggles in her neck, dangling a rosary in his left hand. Cloaked in a flowing regal robe, Madonna and her child are positioned in front of a banner similar to a modern day step and repeat. What catches our eye are two fluttering angels holding up each of the banner's edges not unlike how the Veronica or Shroud have been displayed. That the scene takes place in a rose garden is not accidental. The Blessed Mother has been called the *rosa mystica*, the mystical rose. Recall the three red cinquefoils from the design of the coat of arms for the house of Vergy. They are of the Rosaceae family.

Jan van Eyck's Madonna and Child at the Fountain (1439) | Koninlijk Museum, Antwerp

We see the connection of fountain and the Mother of God reflected in eastern Christianity with the icon of the Panagia, Life-Giving Spring, a feast celebrated on Bright Monday, known as Easter Monday in the west, with legends about miracles and holy wells dating to the fifth century. The imagery also evokes the sacrament of Baptism and healing – the sick are given water from the life-giving spring. In the Gospel of John, Jesus meets a woman from Samaria at Jacob's well. "[T]he water I shall give will become … a spring of water welling up to eternal life."[36] Christ as the font of eternal life is also echoed in the Last Supper, the Eucharist, when Jesus presents the chalice to his disciples: "Drink from it, all of you, for this is my blood of the covenant, which will be shed on behalf of many for the forgiveness of sins."[37]

Mary, the Life-Giving Spring | Χρήστης Templar52, Attribution, via Wikimedia Commons

36 Jn 4:14
37 Mt 26:27-28

The next day, when the spear of Longinus punctuates the side wound we have seen so prominent on Holy Grave sculptures of Christ, blood and water pour forth. An angel collecting the poured out blood and water from the crucified Jesus with a chalice consummates a number of themes explored on our journey, not the least being the figure of Joseph of Arimathea and his association with the battered and bloodied body of Christ. Additionally, we see an Eastern Christian liturgical parallel in both the secular table fountain and the Star of Bethlehem. An asteriskos (or star-cover) is a metal covering that protects the bread from coming into contact with the aer. On censing the asterisk, the priest chants, "And a star came and stood over the place where the young child was,"[38] liturgically linking the Incarnation with the Eucharist.

From a missal leaf, attributed to Nicolo da Bologna (Italian, c. 1325-1403) | Cleveland Museum of Art

Irish philosopher and poet John Scotus Eriugena, who headed the Palace School in the time after Charlemagne during the Carolingian Renaissance, speaks of the wound from Christ's side as "the fount of salvation" cleansing the world clean. In doing so, Christ "ruined death, which had devoured the entire world."[39]

Jean II's son, the duke of Berry, who was not yet sixteen at the Battle of Poitiers, grew to become one of the wealthiest French patrons of the arts, so much so he built his own Sainte Chapelle in Bourges to house a relic of the True Cross and other relics. He commissioned *The Very Rich Hours of the Duke of Berry*, one of the most famous illuminated manuscripts. Work on the manuscript continued after the death of the duke and the manu-

38 Cf. Mt 2:9
39 Celia Chazelle, *The Crucified God in the Carolingian Era* (Cambridge: Cambridge UP, 2001), 202.

script's original painters, the Limbourg Brothers. It eventually came into the possession of Carlo of Savoy, grandson of Louis and Anne of Cyprus, who obtained the Shroud from Magarget de Charny. Carlo, duke of Savoy, and his wife, Blanche of Montferrat, are depicted kneeling in prayer before the Man of Sorrows.

Folio 75r, The Very Rich Hours of the Duke of Berry (Jean Colombe)

In Jean's time, the Limbourg brothers produced *The Fall and the Expulsion from Paradise*. A Gothic fountain rises in the center of the walled island paradise. The visuals offer much to consider, a tableau vivant of Paradise later utilized in Michelangelo's Sistine Chapel, for instance. Yet before the altar is God the Father in a blue cloak passing judgment on Adam and Even, the real fountain of life.[40] In the van Eyck's Ghent Altarpiece, an octagonal-shaped fountain is positioned before the altar of the mystic lamb. The youngest son of King Jean, Philip the Bold, duke of Burgundy, commissioned Claus Sluter for the Well of Moses (1395-1404). A monumental hexagonal column emerging over a deep pool, the fountain was situated in the center of the cloister of Chartreuse de Champmol, the Carthusian monastery and resting place for the Valois dukes of Burgundy, of which Philip was the first.[41] Below the six Old Testament prophets was an entombment scene, unfortunately since destroyed. Positioned twenty-five feet above ground, the mourners clustered around a recumbent Christ, crucified, wounded, and bloodied.[42] Seen in this complete context in which Sluter and his workshop envisioned it, Donna Sadler observed, "the fountain ... was truly unique, for it not only linked the prophecies of Christ's Passion with Calvary, but also functioned as a fountain."[43] This reflected the creative energies and artistic ambition at work by the Burgundian dukes and those around them.

---

40 Cf. Ps 36:10. Also "Sensual Delights: Fountains, Fiction, and Feeling" by Elina Gertsman in *Myth and Mystique*, 59-85, sp. 66.

41 Philip the Bold founded the Carthusian monastery, formally *Chartreuse de la Sainte-Trinité de Champmol*, in 1383. It was dissolved in the French Revolution.

42 Gertsman, 66.

43 Sadler, 32.

PART III
THE WORLD OF
GEOFFROI DE CHARNY

Geoffroi de Charny (c. 1300 – 19 September 1356)

CHAPTER EIGHT

THE PORTABLE ALTAR OF GEOFFROI DE CHARNY

High altars invited further contemplation on moments from the life of Christ. Active in the early 1340s, for example, was Bernat Saulet, a sculptor specializing in alabaster works. Saulet was part of a group of sculptors at Sant Joan de les Abadesses in Catalonia, north of Barcelona. Among the twenty scenes of Christ's life sculpted for an altarpiece (also known as retablos or reredos) by Saulet, still preserved today, is an intimate entombment scene. The Man of Sorrows was also a motif employed for altars, such as Paolo Veneziano's altar screen cover for St. Mark's in Venice in 1345. A decorative textile known as an antependium, an elaborate covering draping an altar's front, often depicted the crucified Christ removed from the cross.

Example of altar retable niche of the entombment, St. Andrew's Church, London | John Salmon, Victorian Web

The Man of Sorrows at the center of Paolo Veneziano's altar screen cover, c. 1345

These visuals of the Passion, lamentation and entombment, whether seen on the altar frontal textile or as alabaster sculptures on a high altar innately drew worshippers into a union with the way of the cross. It is the concept of *kenosis* – a self-emptying of one's own will in favor of complete conformity to the will of God, suffering and the cross included – that is here on display.

All of these motifs culminate in that moment of consecration, the moment of transubstantiation. "[C]entered as it is on the Paschal mystery, the image of Christ is always an icon of the Eucharist, that is, it points to the sacramental presence of the Easter mystery."[1] Sacred relics, in accord with the Council of Nicea (787) were installed in consecrated altars so as to be near the solemn commemoration of Christ's sacrifice that is the Holy Mass. Robert Payne wrote of Pope Urban II, "Heaven was in the relics, and the more relics he possessed the more of heaven lay in his possession."[2] Emmanuel Mouraire, who analyzed Citeaux's high altar reliquary, saw no better place for the relics than where the Eucharist was offered.[3] Of the fifty-three relics in Citeaux's high altar for the dedication of the church of Saint Mary at Citeaux by the bishop of Chalon on November 16, 1193 was a shroud relic that miraculously bled: *De panno ubi corpus Domini involutum fuit miraculose sanguinoletum factum.*[4]

One of the most hallowed of all retablos is the van Eyck brother's early fifteenth-century Adoration of the Mystic Lamb, the Ghent Altarpiece. The sumptuous panels – twelve in total, with the twelfth, that featuring the Mystical Lamb and stolen in 1934 – are contained within double sets of foldable wings. This polyptych device were visual cues for the faithful,

1   Joseph Ratzinger, *The Spirit of the Liturgy* (San Francisco: Ignatius Press, 2000), 133.
2   Payne, *The Dream and the Tomb*, 336.
3   Correspondence with author, June 5, 2019.
4   Emmanuel Mouraire, "Les autels et les reliques de l'abbatiale de Cîteaux" in *Bulletin du centre d'études médiévales d'Auxerre Hors-série* n° 4, 2011, 5.

supplementing the liturgical calendar, and ultimately servicing the Holy Sacrifice consecrated on the main altar before it. Portable altars were also foldable, such as the triptych *Portable Altar with the Madonna and the Saints* featuring the Man of Sorrows, from Venice, late fourteenth century. Others were of stone, such as the Portable Altar of Countess Gertrude, dated to the mid-eleventh century. The Dukes of Burgundy donated a marble portable altar to Citeaux.[5]

Portable Altar with the Madonna and the Saints with Man of Sorrows imagery, late 14th c. | Gallery of the Academy of Fine Arts, Venice

Charny's request to Pope Clement VI (d. 1352, Avignon) for a portable altar was granted in an indult from the pope on June 25, 1344.[6] Along with other indults such as permission for the celebration of liturgies at night and in places under interdict as well as a plenary indulgence in articulo mortis (at the moment of death), the requests reveal a religious man, a knight, frequently on the move, in enemy territory, and in dangerous circumstances, yet not one to abandon reception of the Eucharist. It also implies a retinue that must have included a clerical presence.

Among Geoffroi's inherited lands was the hamlet of Lirey, just outside Troyes in Champagne, which Margaret de Joinville brought to her mar-

5 *Voyage littéraire de deux bénédictins de la Congrégation de Saint-Maur*, Paris, 1717, 222.
6 Pietro Savio, *Ricerche storiche sulla santa Sindone* (Turin: Scuola Grafica Salesiana), (Turin 1957), 234ff.

riage with Jean de Charny at the end of the thirteenth century. It was an ancient Christian land steeped in the legacy of St. Germain of Auxerre (AD 378-448). Local historian Alain Hourseau noted that it was in the vicinity of Lirey where Clovis first set eyes on his future wife and future saint, Clotilde, "on the Roman road, in the small village located at the intersections of the territories of Villery, Lirey and Javernant."[7]

It was here where Geoffroi later realized his long gestating project of building a church, Notre-Dame de Lirey, named specifically in honor of the Annunciation. Following donations received by the king of France, permission obtained from the pope, the administrator of the local parish church, Saint Jean de Bonneval, and abbot of nearby Benedctine abbey, Montier-la-Celle, where St. Robert of Molesme entered the order and St. Bernard of Clairvaux took monastic professions, the wooden church was granted collegiate status, and five canons and a dean were permanently in residence. Charny's vision for the church dated to at least 1343, and records indicate his desire for the memory of his first wife, Jeanne de Toucy-Bazarnes, be remembered with an annual Mass intention on the anniversary of her death.

Although Clement VII, the first Avignon antipope of the Western Schism, later refers to Geoffroi de Charny as so "inflamed by zeal of devotion" he procured a "certain figure or representation of the Sudarium of Our Lord Jesus Christ freely given to him,"[8] Charny himself never mentions such an object. His son, Geoffroi II, and granddaughter, Margaret, only vaguely reference Geoffroi coming into possession of the Shroud in little detail.[9] There is also no evidence of the Shroud in documents related to the foundation of the Lirey church or as an impetus for the building of it. Family churches were common; Geoffroi's grandfather Jean de Joinville, for instance, received permission to establish a family chapel in 1263.[10] Yet the main Joinville chapel was actually a collegiate church, Saint Laurent, recognized as such in 1188 by the lord of Joinville, Geoffroi IV, two years before perishing on the Third Crusade.[11] His son, Geoffroi V, succeeded his father as lord of Joinville and also was a victim on crusade, in 1204.

---

7 Hourseau, 30.

8 "Zelo devotionis accensus" in Bull of Clement VII; Ulyses Chevalier, Autour des origines su suaire de Lirey (Paris: Picard, 1903) Appendix H.

9 "Conquis par feu messire Geoffroy de Charny" is how Marguerite de Charny describes her grandfather procuring the Shroud under oath on 8 May 1449. See Joseph du Teil, "Autour de Saint-Suaire de Lirey" in Bulletin et memoires: Société nationale des antiquaires de France (Paris: C. Klincksieck, 1902), 194n1. Dr. Thomas R. Nevin suggested this translation: "...obtained through armed force by the late Geoffroy de Charny." Nevin continued, "I presume any controversy would be over what force was used and from whom the shroud was wrenched. Hard to believe it was found in the midst of carnage." Correspondence with author, May 7, 2019.

10 Henri-Francois Delaborde, Jean de Joinville et les seigneurs de Joinville (Paris, 1894), 335.

11 Ibid., 34.

Saint Laurent "occupied a position of extraordinary intimacy with the family."[12] In this way, we might be able to see how Geoffroi envisioned Notre-Dame de Lirey by looking further at Saint Laurent. After all, Geoffroi had Joinville blood, built his church on Joinville land, with a surname (Geoffroi) evoking the past lords of Joinville. He was also the beneficiary of his aunt's inheritance, Alix de Beaufort, daughter of Jean de Joinville. Nicholas L. Paul noted, "The chapel of Saint-Laurent was a particularly appropriate place for the family's crusade memorabilia."[13] Jean de Joinville himself relates a story how during the Seventh Crusade (1248-1254), "he made a special journey to the Hospitaller castle of Krak des Chevaliers to collect his uncle Geoffrey V's shield."[14] That shield was eventually placed in the Saint Laurent church, joining saint relics such as those of George, John Chrysostom, and Stephen.[15] The canonization of Jean's own friend, Saint Louis IX, prompted the building of a chapel dedicated to him in Saint Laurent, containing relics of the only canonized French king. Finally, upon his death in 1317, Jean de Joinville was buried in Saint-Laurent.

* * *

Geoffroi's life is remarkably well attested: he first appears in records in 1337 under the count of Eu, Raoul III de Brienne. He was captured at least twice during the Hundred Years' War, the war that would take his life, first at Morlaix by Richard Talbot in 1343, and then again when his plan to retake the port city of Calais failed miserably. Charny attempted to bribe Aimeric di Pavia in allowing French forces to sneak into Calais and surprise the English, who then occupied the city. But di Pavia turned on Charny, alerted Edward III of England and his son, the Black Prince, who lay waiting for the French on the night of December 31, 1349. Following the English route of the French, Edward III took special pleasure in taunting the wounded Charny. An enormous ransom was set for the knight, who earned the honor in 1347 of bearing the French sacred banner, the *oriflamme* (which he would also do in the battle that took his life, at Poitiers in 1356), then spent nearly two years in prison. In due time, in 1352, when governor of Saint-Omer, Charny sought out his betrayer, Aimeric di Pavia, whom he tortured with hot irons. Then he quartered di Pavia with an axe and displayed his body parts above the gates of Fréthun,

---

12 Nicholas L. Paul, *To follow in Their Footsteps: The Crusades and Family Memory in the High Middle Ages* (Ithaca: Cornell UP, 2012), 122.
13 Ibid., 122.
14 Ibid.
15 Jules Simonnet, *Essai sur l'histoire et la généalogie des sires de Joinville, (1008-1386)* (Langres, 1875), 330.

the location outside Calais where di Pavia was seized. Such was the life and times of the first purported owner of the Shroud of Turin.

A few months before his capture at the hands of the English, in response to an April 16, 1349 petition by Charny, Pope Clement's court approved Geoffroi's request that upon his death his body be divided and dispersed in various locales.[16] In a subsequent missive only ten days later from the Avignon court, however, Geoffroi seemed to have changed his mind. Now, he received approval for a new petition, for a cemetery on the church grounds for himself, his family, the church canons, and anyone who so wished.[17] Geoffroi's desire was never realized – he was slain by Reginald Cobham protecting King Jean the Good while clutching the oriflamme at the Battle of Poitiers on September 19, 1356 (one of 2,426 fallen that day). His body was first interred at the nearby house of the Grey Friars before being given a formal funeral fourteen years later by order of King Charles V, Jean's son, at the church of the Celestines in Paris.[18] Also buried there was the heart of his beloved King Jean.[19]

Like most of Catholic France, the church at Lirey (as well as the church of the Celestines) was dissolved in the French Revolution, the building itself demolished in 1828.[20] A small church now stands commemorating the original, and he who built it – lord of Lirey Geoffroi de Charny, knight. In this way, perhaps Geoffroi's initial wish for his remains scattered about Christendom was ultimately realized.

As for the prestigous honor of bearing the oriflamme into battle, the chosen knight accepted it in a solemn ceremony at the monastery of St. Denis, where it was retained during peacetime. We are told:

"Immersed in this atmosphere of candlelight and incense, the guardian of the oriflamme, kneeling with head bared, took the following oath, said out to him by the Abbot of St. Denis: 'You swear and promise *on the precious, sacred body of Jesus Christ present here* and on the bodies of Mon-

---

16 "....post dissolutionem corporis sui, quod idem corpus possit dividi et diversis locis sepeliri"; see Chevalier, Appendix A, 26.

17 Ibid., Appendix B, 27.

18 Richard W. Kaeuper, "Introduction" in *A Knight's Own Book of Chivalry*, trans. Elspeth Kennedy, (Philadelphia: Univ. of Penn Press), 2005, 14.

19 In a poignant gesture of piety, King John, during his imprisonment in England after Poitiers, requested to visit the shrine of Thomas Becket and was granted it: *Anno Domini MCCCLX, dominus Johannes, rex Francourm, postquam in Anglia a festo Inventionis Sanctae Crucix captivatus per triennium remanserat, transitu suo versus Caleys una cum principe Walliae Cantuariam venit, et ibidem ad feretrum Sancti Thomae unum jocale pulcherrimum ad CC marcas et amplius appreciatum, et deinde ad imaginem beatae Mariae in Cryptis unum nowche aureum, pro oblatione dimisit, lapidibus pretiosis ornatum. Et per totum illum diem idem rex in prioratu Cantuariae morabatur.* - *Chronica Johannis de Reading et Anonymi Cantuarensis 1346–1367*, ed. James Tait (Manchester: University Press, 1914), 209.

20 Hourseau, 8.

signeur Saint Denis and his fellows which are here, that you will loyally in person hold and keep the oriflamme of our lord king, who is here, to his honor and profit and that of this realm, and not abandon it for fear of death or whatever else may happen, and you will do your duty everywhere as a good and loyal knight must toward his sovereign and proper lord.'"[21]

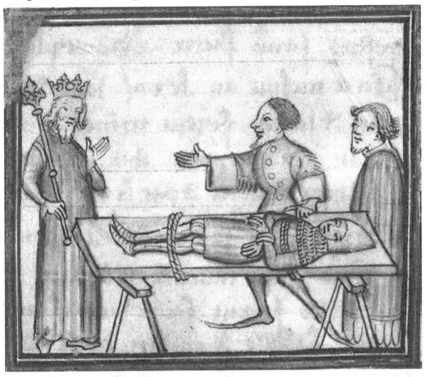

Geoffroi de Charny, captured by the English after the ill-fated siege at Calais, is presented to King Edward III, 1350 (Fleurs des chroniques - Besançon - BM - MS 677 - fol 83)

---

21 Kennedy, 13 (emphasis mine).

Bapst Johannes der drey vñ zweintzigest.

Baldassarre Cossa (c. 1370 – 22 December 1419) Pisan antipope John XXIII (1410–1415)

CHAPTER NINE

THE ANTIPOPE(S)

I t cannot be overlooked that the issue of the Shroud's authenticity rose to the fore in tandem with the Western Schism (1378-1417), which broke western Christendom into two, and eventually, three papal encampments. Earlier in the fourteenth century, Clement V, a stooge for King Philip the Fair and best remembered as the pope who suppressed the Templar Knights, moved the Roman Curia to Avignon in 1309. Six subsequent pontificates ruled from Avignon until Gregory XI, under the influence of Saint Catherine of Siena, returned the Curia to Rome in 1377.

Gregory died the following year. The result of the ensuing conclave was the election on April 9, 1378 of Urban VI (Bartolomeo Prignano), a monk from the Kingdom of Naples. The French cardinalate, displeased with the results, issued a dubia on August 9 about the validity of his election, and on August 20 declared the See of Peter vacant. The French cardinals then held their own conclave outside Rome. Cardinal Robert of Geneva was chosen on September 20, taking the name Clement VII. After a brief sojourn in Naples, Clement VII's version of a papal court returned to the Palais des Papes in Avignon in 1379.[1]

With the blessing from Charles V of France, the Catholic kingdoms of Castile, Aragon, Navarre, Joanna queen of Naples, Flanders, Scotland, Burgundy and Savoy supported Clement. And so in matters related to

Avignon's Palace of the Popes as seen today | Jean-Marc Rosier (http://www.rosier.pro), https://creativecommons.org/licenses/by-sa/3.0/deed.en

---

1 Cox, 319.

the Lirey church, for instance, the bishop of Troyes, Pierre d'Arcis, knight Geoffroi II de Charny and others were seeking papal approval from what history will judge as an antipope.

If not for these wide-reaching implications about the legitimate Successor of Saint Peter, the controversy about a cloth in a country church might be seen as little more than a family quarrel. After all, it was a family affair about a family heirloom: after Geoffroi de Charny's death at Poitiers, his widow, Jeanne de Vergy, remarried Aymon of Geneva, grandson of the Count of Geneva, and second cousin of Clement VII.[2] Years later, when Geoffroi and Jeanne's granddaughter, Margaret, brought the Shroud to the House of Savoy, it was only a few years after the abdication of another antipope, Savoy's Amadeus VIII, who was elected by a faction rivaling both the Avignon and Rome papacies. Taking the name Felix V, his claim to the papal throne gained little traction and he abdicated in 1449. His son and successor to the Savoy dynasty, Louis I, and his wife, Princess Anne of Cyprus, "purchased" the Shroud from Margaret de Charny around March 22, 1453, despite the long-standing prohibition against the sale of relics and the ongoing legal battle with the Lirey canons and Margaret over Shroud ownership.

Sadly, Margaret's legal tussles with the canons resulted in her excommunication, a humiliating social taboo in the Middle Ages. And a spiritual one – Margaret died in 1460, her excommunication having never been lifted.

As for Pope Clement VII, he did not limit his ambitions to his supported regions alone: he sought nothing less than to unseat Urban VI and declare the Schism over and he the victorious pontiff. When Urban VI deposed Joanna from the Naples throne upon her loyalty shifting to Clement, Clement saw the ideal political inciting incident to accomplish this goal. He turned to his cousin, the Green Count of Savoy, Amadeus VI. Along with Louis, duke of Anjou, Clement persuaded both to overturn the kingdom of Naples in their favor and march on to expel Urban VI from Rome and "remove the poison from the Holy Church."[3] The plan did not come to fruition, but it reveals seething animosity towards Rome from Clement. As Clement in Avignon debated how to pacify the bishop of Troyes and his kinsman in Lirey over the exhibition of the Shroud, Urban VI in Rome announced a Holy Year for 1390, and surely the Roman Veronica would again be displayed. Clement responded in November

---

2 Nicolotti, 103, n.86.
3 Ibid., 328.

1389 by threatening excommunication on anyone under his obedience who journeyed to Rome for it. It was not novel, however, to issue such a command. For the Holy Year of 1350, Edward III of England discouraged his subjects from attending, fearing the amount of money leaving his domain.[4]

For that jubilee year, Herbert Thurston, SJ estimated that from Christmas 1349 through Easter 1350, 1.2 million pilgrims passed through Rome. "The Volto Santo or Sudario, the napkin believed to have been offered to our Saviour by Saint Veronica, and to have retained the impression of His sacred countenance, was shown at Saint Peter's on every Sunday and Feast day, at which time the multitudes who thronged the church were so great that many were suffocated or trampled to death."[5]

Left: Exhibition of the Roman Veil of Veronica; woodcut from Mirabilia Urbis Romae; (2) King Louis IX displays Passion relics in Ostension of the Crown of Thorns, stained glass, 1241-1245, Sainte-Chapelle, Paris; (3) Ostension of the Holy Shroud, Christophe Duche, 1559

Quoting an eyewitness from the 1390 Holy Year, Thurston wrote, "We are told that the desire of beholding the Supreme Pontiff again in his ancient see contributed something towards attracting pilgrims."[6] Such a sentiment, if it got back to Clement VII, would not have gone over well. But by 1390, Clement had effectively abandoned his dream of defeating the Roman pontiff as he gradually lost support. He died four years later.

---

4   Herbert Thurston, *SJ, The Holy Year of Jubilee: An Account of the History and Ceremonial of the Roman Jubilee* (London: Sand & Co., 1900); 57, n. 1.

5   Thurston, 58.

6   Thurston, 63 citing Torsellino, *Storia Lauretana*, lib. i. cap. 21.

The memorial of Bishop Pierre d'Arcis from 1389 in which the Shroud, which recently appeared in Lirey, is cited and its claim to authenticity is denounced. See Appendix A.

CHAPTER TEN

A PLACE OF PILGRIMAGE

The Shroud was the subject of controversy from its first reliable entry in the historical record when Troyes bishop Pierre d'Arcis (d. 1395) drafted a long complaint to Clement VII presumably in the second half of 1389 that "a short while ago in the diocese of Troyes, the dean of a certain collegiate church, specifically in Lirey, deceitfully and wickedly, inflamed with the fire of avarice and cupidity, not from devotion but for gain, arranged to have in his church a certain cloth, cunningly portrayed, on which was portrayed in a subtle manner the double image of a single man, that is to say his front and back; [the dean] falsely asserted and pretended that this was the very shroud in which our Savior Jesus Christ was enrobed in the sepulchre, and on which shroud there had remained the impression of the whole likeness of the Savior himself with the wounds that he bore."[1]

D'arcis goes on to mention that his predecessor, Henri de Poitiers (d. 1370) actually located the cloth's artist. As a result, the dean and canons hid the cloth in a secret place, but now, more than thirty years later, Geoffroi II de Charny was urged by the current dean of Notre-Dame de Lirey to resume expositions of the cloth "and the church would be enriched by the proceeds."[2] Geoffroi, a knight just like his esteemed father, sought permission from papal nuncio Cardinal de Thury, according to d'Arcis. The exhibitions of the Shroud resumed, proclaimed in public it was a figure or representation of the true burial shroud of Christ. d'Arcis claims, however, that "in private it is asserted and proclaimed [as the true shroud], and so it is believed by many."[3]

d'Arcis mentions the Shroud was displayed "on solemn feast days, and otherwise, openly, with the greatest solemnity, even greater than when the Body of our Lord Jesus Christ was shown there." Feasts mentioned in earlier documents from the Avignon court grant indulgences to faithful and pilgrims who visit Notre Dame de Lirey include the Nativity of the

---

1 See English translation in Nicolotti, 90-96; Chevalier, Etude critique, doc G. The English translation of d'Arcis's draft letter to Clement can be found in the Appendix.
2 Ibid.
3 Ibid.

Lord, Circumcision, Epiphany, Parasceves, Easter, the Ascension, Pentecost, Trinity Sunday, Corpus Christi, and others.[4]

d'Arcis then describes how the Shroud was exhibited: "two priests garbed in albs with stoles and maniples, very reverently, with torches lit and in a high elevated place built especially for this alone."[5] This description resembles a palm-sized bronze pilgrim badge found in the mud during excavations of the Seine River under the Pont-au-Change bridge in Paris in 1855. It shows a depiction of the Shroud in a horizontal position. Above, fragments of two prelates, their heads missing, clutch the Shroud wearing stoles doubled over and clasped together, resembling the Saint Andrew's Cross (x-shaped design). This shape suggests they are canons, and not bishops or other hierarchy. Flanking the cloth are two pillars, suggesting the cloth was mounted or affixed to them in exhibition. Certainly, it was meant to show an interior church setting.

The Lirey Pilgrim Badge

Below the cloth, on the badge's left side, as we have already seen, is the Charny family coat of arms depicting three silver escutcheons (shields). On the right, a second coat of arms, that of Vergy: three red cinquefoils, a shape of flowers gardeners will identify with the family *Rosaceae*. Heraldry exploded in popularity in the medieval period, utilized on battle gear to expression

4 Chevalier, *Etude critique*, doc. C, D, E.
5 Chevalier, *Etude critique*, doc. G.

of ownership and status. Researchers commonly conclude that these specific coat of arms on the badge suggest it must have been struck during the time during or after the marriage between Geoffroi de Charny and Jeanne de Vergy. Yet as evident in Jean de Joinville's quest to bring his uncle's shield back from Syria, medieval memories were long, and family ties were proudly remembered in heraldry. It was not until 1418 when, under the threat of war and looting, the Shroud and other relics were ushered out of Lirey by Humbert de Villersexel, leaving open the possibility the pilgrim badge was struck under the lordship of Geoffroi II de Charny (d. 1398) or his daughter, the last Charny owner of the Shroud, Margaret. (It is worth noting that eventually all the relics were returned to Notre-Dame de Lirey – except the Shroud.)

Between the coat of arms on the Lirey badge are the *arma Christi*, visuals of the instruments of the Passion, a motif dating to the sixth century.[6] Here, whips flank a nimbus-like roundel, inside of which a cross, with the crown of thorns as around it as like a laurel wreath, rises out of an empty tomb. In this tiny amulet the commemoration of a Shroud exhibit is clear.

While the facts on how the Shroud actually appeared in Lirey remains elusive, this rather sophisticated pilgrim badge displays an understanding of contemporary Passion imagery, and combined with the blasons of the house of Charny and Vergy serves as a sort of marketing tool to draw pilgrims towards its exhibitions. The inclusion of the *arma Christi* also evokes, from a Church calendar perspective, the most important dates of the year – the Triduum.

Additionally, the visualization of the tools used in the Passion were considered "signs in shorthand" to the medieval mind. German art historian Robert Suckale correlated the instruments of the Passion as examples of what Aquinas termed *signa rememorativa*, a way to instantly recall something from the past, in this case, the sufferings and death of Christ.[7] Nor was such imagery for decorative purposes only. Pope Innocent IV granted indulgence status to the *arma Christi* at the Council of Lyon in 1245,[8] the same pontiff "who granted the single largest indulgence, one year and 100 days, to visitors of the Sainte-Chapelle."[9] The Shroud as it was installed in Lirey, with its approved indulgences by Innocent VI, also falls under the categorization of *signa rememorativa*.

---

6 Heather Madar, "Iconography of Sign: A Semiotic Reading of the Arma Christi" in *ReVisioning: Critical Methods of Seeing Christianity in the History of Art*, ed. James Romaine and Linda Stratford (Eugene: Cascade Books, 2013), 117.

7 Timmerman, 227.

8 Madar, 118.

9 Meredith Cohen, "An Indulgence for the Visitor: The Public at the Sainte-Chapelle of Paris" in *Speculum*, vol. 83, no. 4 (Oct. 2008), 867.

Example of arma Christi, the instruments of the Passion (British Library MS 37049)

In 2009 a metal mould (template) of a Shroud pilgrim's badge was evidently found by a jogger in Machy, a mile from Lirey.[10] It is nearly identical to the Lirey badge but with a few differences: a face is visible for one of the two prelates with crossed stoles; the two side pillars are again present, and now apparent are two trefoil (or trilobe) arches behind the clerics. There is no *arma Christi* on this mould. Instead, below the horizontal display of the scraped-away two-figured cloth, is a Veronica – the holy face of Christ. On either side of the face, once again, the coat of arms of the families Charny and Vergy. Only this time, they are reversed, with Vergy's on the left and Charny's on the right. Below the face of Christ, the capital letters S U A I R E : ι η V. *Suaire* – French for "shroud," and the Greek letters for Christ. There also appears to be the initial E and on the right C, though they are ultimately unclear. Various ideas have been suggested. One could be they are abbreviations for *Ecce concipies*, the archangel Gabriel's foretelling to Mary from St. Luke's Gospel of the Incarnation: "Behold, you shall conceive…", connecting the badge with the name of the Charney church in Lirey, Our Lady of the Annunciation.

10 Alain Hourseau, *Autour du Saint Suaire et de la collegiale de Lirey* (Aube, 2012).

In any case, while these badges do not reveal the origins of the Shroud itself, a conflation of multiple themes come together in these tiny details that indicate the intention of whoever commissioned them. We might even recall the imprint of Christ's face on communion hosts, let alone the bust of Christ on Veronica's cloth, echoed here on the mould. Whatever its true origins, it resembles a later Shroud pilgrim badge during the Savoy era:

Artist's rendering of the Shroud "Machy mould" found in 2009, left, and a pilgrim badge of the Shroud from the 16th century, right. Note the similar "SUAIRE"

These badges pack numerous motifs all united under the umbrella of Passion devotion as if to say, here is the object of the Passion: the sarcophagus and instruments of the Passion, the Veronica icon of the face of Christ, the duality of Christ's humanity and divinity, the liturgical component of commemorating the sacrifice of Christ's suffering and death, and finally the image of the crucified himself. In this way, these pilgrim badges take on greater meaning and significance than the linen cloth itself.

Pilgrim badges and amulets remain a trademark for those who embark on a certain pilgrimage – consider the shell for those undertaking the Camino de Santiago. The Veronica image was one such souvenir. A Veronica badge dated c. 1325-1375 was found in Sluis, Netherlands, and an aged pilgrim with both the Veronica and Camino scallop shell constitutes part of Andrea di Bonaiuti's fresco of the Militant and Triumphant Church, c. 1365. The Holy Years of 1300 and 1350, in which the Roman Veronica was the major draw, provided opportunities to spread the Veronica cult elsewhere throughout Christendom through the sale of Veronica souvenirs and Veronica painted images.[11]

---

11 Wolff, 173.

The Camino de Santiago loomed large in the medieval mind; it is impossible not to underestimate its popularity. Pope Callixtus II (d. 1124) instituted the Compostela Holy Years, celebrated whenever the Feast of Saint James (July 25) fell on a Sunday. In 1137, William X of Aquitaine died while on pilgrimage along the Camino, making his twelve-year-old daughter, Eleanor, duchess of Aquitaine. A certain individual named Guillaume de Charny and his wife, Jehan, donated to L'hopital de Saint-Jacques, a hospital in Paris devoted to pilgrims of the Chemin de Saint Jacques in 1298.[12] The Joinville-Charny fief of Lirey straddled both Champagne and Burgundy, in the diocese of Troyes while beholden to the dukes of Burgundy at Isle-Aumont. The location was central to draw pilgrims along the nearby Via Francigena en route to Rome or the Holy Land, and those along the Frankish routes of the Camino de Santiago. For instance, the church of Saint Lazarus in the Burgundian village of Avallon brought pilgrims eager to glimpse the relic of Lazarus while bound for Vézelay, the launch point of the Via Lemovicensis, with final destination nothing less than the Saint James Cathedral at Santiago de Compostela nearly nine hundred miles away. Vézelay was the location sought by *jacquets* (French pilgrims of the Camino) coming from Flanders, Champagne, and Alsace.

In the thirteenth century, Jean de Brienne (d. 1237), the king of Jerusalem and later emperor of Constantinople (who contemporary sources like Matthew Paris indicated he lived out his days as a Franciscan friar in Constantinople), Raymond VII, count of Toulouse (d. 1249), and Hugh IV, duke of Burgundy, son of the powerful duchess consort Alix de Vergy, were just some of the names from Champagne-Burgundy in the thirteenth century who took up the pilgrim's stick.[13] On King Louis IX's deathbed in Tunis in North Africa, succumbing to the dysentery that besieged those on the Seventh Crusade, he mentioned by name Saint James.[14]

Right, a group of pilgrims with their walking sticks. Note the Veronica icon of Christ and Camino shell on man's hat

---

12 Henri Léonard Bordier, *La confrérie des pèlerins de Saint-Jacques: et ses archives* (Paris: Société des antiques de France, 1860), 190.

13 See V.L.C., "Aimeric Picaudi de Parthenai" in *Cantique des Pelerins* (Paris: Firmin Didot, 1847), 289.

14 Delaborde, 16.

Jean de Joinville, while on Saint Louis's first crusade to Egypt in 1248, implored the protection of Saint James during a surprise Saracen attack: "Monseigneur Erard de Siverey was struck by a sword-blow in his face, so that his nose hung down over his lips. And then I was minded of Monseigneur Saint Jacques, whom I thus invoked: 'Beau Sire Saint Jacques, help and succor me in this need.'"[15] Devotion to the apostle James, known as the Greater, was evident in the Joinville family by the donation of Jean de Joinville's grandfather, Geoffroi IV, when he confirmed the founding of the Saint James priory on Joinville land.[16]

A stopover after Vézelay on the Via Lemovicensis is a small commune named after its church, now a basilica, Neuvy-Saint-Sepulchre. Cardinal Eudes de Châteauroux was largely responsible for rebuilding the church into a replica of Jerusalem's Church of the Holy Sepulcher. Originally named for Saint James, the church as it was redesigned would have served pilgrims as another *signa rememorativa*, a remembrance of the original Way, that of Christ's own pilgrimage to Calvary. A companion of St. Louis and Jean de Joinville on the king's crusade to Egypt, Odo de Châteauroux was close enough to Louis that he was chosen to consecrate the Sainte-Chapelle in 1248. Châteauroux was also largely responsible for preaching the crusade King Louis eventually led, per orders of Pope Innocent IV. Châteauroux donated drops of Christ's blood to Neuvy-Saint-Sepulchre and actual stones from the Jerusalem sepulcher in 1254.[17]

Farther south off the Via Lemovicensis was yet another major pilgrimage destination, the Cistercian abbey of Cadouin. Known in the Middle Ages for possessing another cloth claimed to be from the Holy Sepulcher, it drew peasant and royal alike, including King Philippe VI in 1335. In 1399, mad King Charles VI demanded the cloth be brought to him in order that gazing upon it might cure him of his own insanity.[18]

The home of Geoffroi de Charny's paternal ancestral line, Mont-Saint-Jean, was also just off the Vézelay route, with a portion of its monstrous castle serving as a hospital, a hotel-Dieu ("hostel for God") for needy villagers and pilgrims. Curiously, a number of crosses are emblazoned on various buildings around the property, identified as the Maltese-style crosses of the order of knights of Saint Jean of Jerusalem, the Knights Hospitaller.[19] The local church of Mont-Saint-Jean was named after Saint

---

15 Henry Osborn Taylor, *The Medieval Mind* (New York: The MacMillan Company, 1919), 562.
16 Delaborde, 35.
17 Colin Morris, *The Sepulchre of Christ and the Medieval West* (Oxford: Oxford UP, 2005), 160.
18 Dor, 93.
19 See "Mont-Saint-Jean," https://bourgognemedievale.com/departement-et-pays/cote-dor/pays-auxois-morvan-cote-dorient/mont-saint-jean/.

John the Baptist, one of the military order's patron saints. Thirty miles to the south of Mont-Saint-Jean sits the Château de Bellecroix, former commandery of the Hospitallers. Indeed, documentation exists of land agreements and other negotiations between the Hospitallers and the lords of Mont-Saint-Jean.[20] The order's seal is not entirely clear, but it appears to show a figure wrapped in bandages, hands crossed over pelvis. Donna Sadler, for one, identified it as the dead Christ.[21] If the Templars' primary function was protection for the pilgrims to the Holy Land and defense of the Holy Sepulcher, the Hospitallers were formed to tend to the sick among the pilgrims so they could worship within Christendom's most hallowed shrine. Prior to Latin control of Jerusalem, the Eastern Orthodox order Brotherhood of the Holy Sepulcher guarded the church.

Seal of the Knights Hospitallers

Other local tales developed revolving around villages, churches and abbeys designed to attract pilgrims en route to connect with the main

---

20 *Inventaire Sommaire des Archives départementales: Yonne*, t. IV (Auxerre, 1897), 17, 20, 24, 209.
21 Sadler, 88n287.

Camino roads, a sort of medieval version of a "tourist trap." Between Lyon and Valence off the Rhône, for example, is the Plan de l'Aiguille, the Pyramid, a remnant from the Roman occupation. In the 1200s, a story circulated that the pyramid marked the tomb of Pontius Pilate,[22] where he was exiled in disgrace for his involvement with the death of the Messiah. Second century Church father Tertullian implied Pilate ultimately converted to Christianity "in conscience."[23]

Interactions with fellow believers throughout Christendom, then, were not only inevitable but commonplace. German and Alsace pilgrims, long immersed in Grail lore permeated by the poetry of Wolfram von Eschenbach (d. 1220) and later from other Minnesang such as Konrad von Würzburg, did not limit their particular expressions of faith to geography alone but shared their devotions with those they encountered. We will see a critical instance of this merging later with the dukes of Burgundy and early Netherlandish painters from present-day Belgium, a merger which involved the family Charny.

The Hundred Years' War reshaped the pilgrim tradition from France to Santiago de Compostela. The English presence in the kingdom no longer made such pious excursions safe. Centuries passed before the pilgrim routes were rediscovered. Today, the Camino is widely popular as both a religious pilgrimage and a secular journey. The Cathedral of Saint James remains the final destination.

---

22 Jacques Berlioz, "Crochet de fer et puits à tempêtes: La légende de Ponce Pilate à Vienne (Isère) et au mont Pilat au XIIIe siècle" in *Le Monde alpin et rhodanien* (1990), 85–104.
23 Tibor Grüll, "The Legendary Fate of Pontius Pilate" in *Classica et Mediaevalia* 61, 151–176, 166.

St. Veronica, Lorenzo Costa (attributed to), 1508 - Louvre Museum

Chapter Eleven

Archways & Peacocks

Before finding new owners in the House of Savoy, Margaret de Charny took the Shroud on the road, gradually establishing a reputation for the Shroud that would only grow. The Shroud spent some time in properties held by her second husband, Count Humbert de Villersexel, in the idyllic village of Saint Hippolyte on France's modern eastern border, mere miles from the Rhine River. A fifteenth century fresco found in Saint Leger Church in nearby Terres de Chaux suggested a commemoration, or at least knowledge, of the Shroud's existence in the Doubs region. For our purposes here, however, the architectural placement of the fresco might lend some further insight.

The arch at the entrance to the apse of Saint Leger is a type of arch called a triumphal arch, a holdover from Roman architecture. A communion rail remains in place under it. The faint mosaic over the arch shows two angels flanking the arch each clutching the ends of a winding sheet, which runs over the top of the arch. This is seen from the nave and transept. On the arch's other side, that is, looking up at the arch from within the sanctuary, there is a Veronica depiction: below two full-size angels blowing trumpets, two figures clutch a towel showing only Christ's head within a nimbus. The inclusion of these figures in these locations confirmed the symbolic importance of the transition from transept to sanctuary, from one reality to a heightened reality, one in which time collapsed, and God Himself humbly appeared on altar tops and before soaring retablos.

Sanctuary of Saint Leger, Terres des Chaux | Sacamol, Under Creative Commons license, https://creativecommons.org/licenses/by-sa/4.0/

Rumors of the Shroud in Greece before it arrived in Champagne have long been a favorite of those promoting the hypothetical route of the Shroud from Constantinople to France. Noel Currer-Briggs and others identified the Acheiropoietos Basilica in Thessaloniki as a logical place for the Shroud to be kept during this period of its journey. For Currer-Briggs, the very name of the basilica, Acheriopoietos, "not made by human hands," was a clue.[1] The original church name, founded in the second half of the fifth century, was Panagia Theotokos, after the Virgin Mary. The name change for Currer-Briggs suggested it was "not unbelievable to believe that the [Shroud] was installed there during this period."[2]

The early mosaics from this basilica were studied by Dr. Konstantinos Raptis of the Hellenic Ministry of Culture and Sports in Thessaloniki.[3] Dr. Raptis effectively debunked the idea that the name of the basilica was a veiled Shroud reference, indicating "acheiropoietos" referred to a liturgical icon of the Virgin.[4] Upon inspection of art within the basilica, a series of mosaics cannot be overlooked. Dr. Raptis described them as "elaborate geometrical patterns, like interlacing polychrome bands, meanders, and fish-scale patterns with peacock-feather eyelets, variable vegetative snytheses with vines, ears, nymphaeas, lilies, oral or fruitful leafy garlands, and acanthus shaped candelabras as well."[5]

Acheiropoietos Basilica intrados mosaic, Thessaloniki, 5th c.
Courtesy Konstantinos Raptis

These were mosaics in arch intradoses, the inner curve of an arch. Three of these mosaics in the gallery arcade all featured a Latin cross in

---

1 Noel Currer-Briggs, *The Shroud and the Grail* (New York: Saint Martin's Press, 1987). 151. Also, Currer-Briggs, "The Shroud in Greece" (London: British Society for the Turin Shroud, 1988).
2 Ibid.
3 Konstantinos T. Raptis, "Acheiropoietos Basilica: architecture and sculptural decoration," Ph.D dissertation. Aristotle University of Thessaloniki, 2016. volume I, chapter II.B.4, pp. 83-97.
4 Correspondence with author, January 28, 2019.
5 Konstantinos T. Raptis, "The Mural Decoration of Acheiropoietos Basilica Revisited" in *Niš and Byzantium, Twelfth Symposium, The collection of scientific works XII*, 2014, 103-104.

the center of two matching lush plants, the heads of peacocks – an early Christian symbolism for eternal salvation – swarming around the cross.

The evocative duality of the plant imagery mirrored the duality of the frontal and dorsal body images on the Shroud, suggesting deeper symbolic meaning particularly in relation to arches and doorways. The symmetry was impeccable with these intrados mosaics, as well as in the images above the triumphal arch at Saint Leger, for instance, or the royal doors of an iconostasis.

Along this theme of duality is the harmony of the gold cherubim on the Ark of the Covenant as detailed in the Book of Exodus: "The cherubim shall have their wings spread out above, sheltering the cover with them; they shall face each other, with their faces looking toward the cove."[6] For Saint Bernard of Clairvaux, the true ark of the covenant was the womb of the Virgin, whose fruit, Christ, was the flesh that gave life to the world. This, then, was the ark of the Resurrection, the new covenant.

Above, James Tissot's rendition of the Ark of the Covenant, c. 1900; below, cover image for Michele Berod's Le prerogatiue della santissima Sindone in compendio, 1648

6 Ex 25:20

Less than a mile from Acheiropoietos in Thessaloniki is the church of Saint Nicholas Orphanos. Built in the second decade of the 1300s, the church's fresco-packed interior features the mandylion above a Roman arch panel of the Blessed Mother flanked by two identical and bowing angels. This style of the mandylion matches nearly exactly the mandylion seen in the pendentive of the King's Church in central Serbia, named after King Stefan Uroš II Milutin and built in 1313. These identical mandylion are not coincidental: among the various churches King Milutin commissioned was Saint Nicholas Orphanos in Thessaloniki.

We might again recall the epitaphios of King Stefan Uroš II Milutin. Let us look at another epitaphios, likely produced from a workshop in Thessaloniki itself, circa 1300. We recognize the features of the dead Christ, atop a shroud with prominent zig zag lines. We see familiar imagery of angelic wheels, wings, and four angels behind the Christ looking down at the crucified savior similar to the Three Marys and mourners of entombment scenes. The two angel-deacons appear to be holding communion plates. Indeed, the Greek inscription reads: *Drink from it, all of you; for this is my blood of the covenant; Take, eat, this is my body.*[7]

Epitaphios cloth, circa 1300 A.D. (Museum of Byzantine Culture, Thessaloniki)

---

7 Byzantium: Faith and Power, 187A, 312.

CHAPTER TWELVE

THE CHARNYS AND PASSION ART

The family Charny loyally served the dukes of Burgundy, even before Jean II brought the duchy of Burgundy under the French crown with his marriage to Joan of Auvergne. In 1313, the sixteen-year-old duke, Louis, received the principality of Achaea from Philip I of Taranto upon Louis's marriage to Matilda of Hainaut. Although this was years after the Latin hold on Constantinople, Thessaloniki, and the Morea, the west still maintained a presence through a number of Frankish baronies. Matilda and Louis's time in Achaea to lay claim to their possessions was disastrous for both. Within three years, Louis was dead, but not before marrying off one of his knights, Dreux de Charny, brother of Geoffroi I de Charny, to the baroness of Vostitza, Agnes de Charpigny.[1]

Andrea Nicolotti discovered a document from June 30, 1346 mentioning both Geoffroi and his nephew, Philippe de Jonvelle, son-in-law of Dreux and Agnes.[2] This was twenty years after Dreux's death, suggesting a close relationship between uncle and nephew. Philippe married Agnes and Dreux's daughter, Guillemette, two years earlier. In 1359 Guillemette sold the baronies of Vostitza and Nivelet to Marie of Bourbon and her husband, Robert of Taranto, titular prince of Achaea and titular Latin emperor of Constantinople.[3]

Robert had another title to his name – king of Albania. This seemingly obscure regal claim suggests a potential interlocking of people and places important in our journey. Though conjectural, nevertheless what follows does imply a strong dynamic between the Orthodox east and Latin west that supposedly looked at one another as mortal enemies. The brother of St. Louis IX, Charles of Anjou (d. 1285), king of Jerusalem and king of Sicily, styled himself king of Albania and entered into alliance with the kings of Bulgaria and Serbia, a pact bolstered by the marriage of his relative, Helen of Anjou, and Stefan Uroš I. The anti-Orthodox sentiment of the Angevin was a direct affront to the Second Council of Lyon (1274),

---

1 Antoine Bon, *The Frankish Morea. Historical, Topographic and Archaeological Studies on the Principality of Achaea* (Paris: De Boccard, 1969), 464.
2 Nicolotti, 74, n.25.
3 Ferdinand Aldenhoven, *Itineraire descriptif de l'attique et du Peloponese* (Athens: 1841), XIII.

when Pope Gregory X contemplated assenting to Byzantine emperor Michael VIII's desire for Orthodox and Catholic reunification. But Charles and his papal stooge, Martin IV (reigned from 1281-1285), had no interest in such an endeavor. Thus, Greek fear of a Latin invasion was palpable – including from those on the hallowed grounds of Mt. Athos. The king of Albania title was assumed by his son, Charles II, his son, Philip I of Taranto, and his son, Robert of Taranto, husband of Marie de Bourbon. Marie's younger brother, as it turned out, was a member of the Order of the Star – Jacques de la Marche, who was taken prisoner at Poitiers. Her father was Louis, duke of Bourbon, another member of the order.

This tangential discourse in genealogy is to suggest, again only speculatively, a potential link in east and west relations that may have something to do with the origins of the Shroud and its placement in the Charny-Vergy church. Helen of Anjou, great-niece of the last ruling Latin emperor of Constantinople, Baldwin II, and whose grandmother was the ex-empress, Maria of Hungary, founded the Gradac Monastery where Noel Currer-Briggs thought he saw the Grail/Shroud in the monastery church's mandylion fresco. Helen was also, it is remembered, the mother of Stefan Uroš II. As we saw earlier, the epitaphios bearing his name is unmistakably similar to the Shroud. The Serbian alliance with Albania extended to the Morea through Robert of Taranto and his wife, Marie of Bourbon. When Guillemette de Jonvelle dispossessed her baronies, her daughter, Agnes de Jonvelle was still married to her first husband, Guillaume de Vergy.

It is in this relationship, Agnes de Jonvelle and Guillaume de Vergy, where the strands of this lost world come together.

Guillaume's parents were Jean de Vergy and Isabeau de Joinville, granddaughter of Jean de Joinville and half-sister to Dreux and Geoffroi de Charny. Guillaume's great-grandfather, Jean de Vergy, is also the great-grandfather of Geoffroi II de Charny. In turn, Guillaume's father, Jean, was half-brother of Jeanne de Vergy, second wife of Geoffroi de Charny and mother of Geoffroi II. While the close ties are not uncommon in medieval marriage, clearly we see an inter-alliance of certain families. This is even further amplified when we see that after Guillaume's death, Agnes remarried, to Philibert de Bauffremont. Their first child, Jean, married Margaret de Charny, who gave the Shroud to the Savoy.

The linchpin here is Agnes de Jonvelle. Not only was she the mother-in-law of Margaret de Charny and granddaughter of Vostitza barons Dreux and Agnes, but she was also the grandmother of Pierre de Bauffremont (1397-1472). Pierre, the count of Charny, was husband to Marie of Burgundy, legitimized daughter of the duke of Burgundy, Philip the Good. Here again we see a close alliance with the dukes, dating to duke Odo III's marriage with Alix de Vergy (d. 1252). Pierre, who joined Philip the Good's Order of the Fleece, depicted on his shield the coat of arms of his ancestors: Bauffremont, Charny, and Vergy. Additionally, we are told Philip was godfather to the daughter of Jan van Eyck, "who the chamberlain de Charny held at the font,"[4] suggesting Pierre de Bauffremont was the duke's proxy at the baptism.

Pierre de Bauffremont and his coat of arms showing both his Charny and Vergy heritage

The legacy of Agnes de Jonvelle-Bauffremont today lives on in Los Angeles, California. The limestone sculpture *Panels from the Retable of Agnes de Beauffremont*, part of the William Randolph Hearst Collection, is owned by the Los Angeles County Museum of Art (LACMA). A similar limestone work, *Retable with Scenes of the Passion*, is kept in Boston's Gardner Museum. The niche of the Three Marys in both works, with sleeping guards underneath, is identical in similar retables by the same workshop. What is striking about the lamentation niche is the missing body of Christ, what Donna Sadler refers to as the "absent presence of Christ."[5]

---

4   J.A. Crowe and G.B. Calvacaselle, *The Early Flemish Painters* (London: John Murray, 1872), 99.
5   See Sadler, Ch. 3 in *Stone Flesh Spirit*, "The Entombment of Christ: The Absent Presence of the

Retable with Scenes of the Passion with Christ absent in entombment niche

The description by the Gardner Museum tells us the retable was created for Guillaume Bouvenot and his wife, Gudelette. These donors also sponsored a nearly identical retable in the St. Barbara chapel in the church of St. Etienne in Vignory, fifty miles east of Troyes but only just over ten miles south of Joinville. "The activity of this workshop at Vignory is attested … by the Bouvenot altar," a 1977 Gardner museum book noted. "Nevertheless, the more important town of Joinville has been proposed as the more probable center of its activity."[6] Speaking of the Gardner retable Donna Sadler remarked, "This retable is thought to be the finest work of the Joinville-Vignory atelier, a sculptor and his workshop that resided in Champagne, but was deeply influenced by both Burgundian and Flemish art."[7] Helga Hoffmann pegged the years of flourishing for the workshop as 1393-1442.[8]

Resurrected Christ and the Holy Sepulcher"

6 "109. Retable with Scenes of the Passion" in Sculpture in the Isabella Stewart Gardner Museum (Boston: 1977), 81.

7 Donna L. Sadler, *Touching the Passion – Seeing the Late Medieval Altarpieces Through the Eyes of Faith* (Leiden: Brill, 2018), 117.

8 Helga D. Hoffmann, "L'atelier de sculpture de Joinville-Vignory" in *Bulletin Monumental*, tome 127, n°3, année 1969, 209- 222.

The evidence for the Joinville connection with the workshop dates to the will of Marguerite, countess of Joinville, who on June 15, 1387, ordered twin tombs for herself and her husband, the duke of Lorraine, to be constructed in the Joinville church, Saint-Laurent. Unfortunately, the French Revolution spared neither the tombs nor the church.[9]

It should also be noted that the prayer book of Philip the Bold (d. 1404) "contains six inserted Veronicas, not all of them additions, and originally contained many more,"[10] and that his grandson, Philip the Good, is the one to have included them. So consumed was Philip the Good it is thought he physically ingested paint chips off the faces of Christ.[11]

At this very time entombment sculptures populated Christendom. In Burgundy, a prominent element to these tableaus was the burial cloth of Christ. We see this particularly in the entombment at Hôtel-Dieu de Tonnerre. Located twenty miles directly south of Lirey on the pilgrim trail to Santiago de Compostela, Hôtel-Dieu de Tonnerre was founded as a hospital in 1293 by the ruling countess of Tonnerre, Margaret of Burgundy. Margaret was also the widow of Charles of Anjou, who died in 1285. During her final years in Tonnerre, Margaret lived a quasi-monastic life with two other women, Margaret of Brienne and Catherine, recognized Latin empress of Constantinople and princess of Achaea living in exile in Burgundy – and future grandmother of Robert of Taranto.

Entombment scene with prominent shroud folds, Hôtel-Dieu de Tonnerre, Burgundy, c. 1454 | Paul Hermans, CC BY-SA 4.0 <https://creativecommons.org/licenses/by-sa/4.0>

9 Ibid., 211.
10 Jeffrey F. Hamburger, *The Visual and the Visionary: Art and Female Spirituality in Late Medieval Germany* (New York: Zone Books, 1998), 329.
11 Kathryn M. Rudy, "Eating the Face of Christ: Philip the Good and his Physical Relationship with Veronicas" in *The European Fortune of the Roman Veronica,* ed. Amanda Murphy (Brno: Convivium, 2017), 169-178.

Images of Christ's entombment within a hospital setting further emphasizes the theme of the afflicted and infirmed finding empathy in the passion and death of Christ, with the hope of eternal glory through the resurrection. The rector of the Tonnerre hospital at the time of the entombment's installation was Brother Pierre Crapillet of the Order of the Holy Ghost, the order which served the hospital. It was also an order based in Rome, at Santo Spirito in Sassia, the same location where Pope Innocent III processed with the Roman Veronica in 1208 – and a hospital largely paid for by Innocent III himself. Another hospital run by the Order of the Holy Ghost in Burgundy was in Dijon. It was established around 1204 by the duke of Burgundy, Odo III, wife of Alix de Vergy.

All this indicates the Joinville-Charny-Jonvelle-Vergy-Bauffremont family supported an artistic workshop that contributed to the wider movement of early Netherlandish artists, the patrons of whom were the dukes of Burgundy, and creators of some of the works we have already explored. While one can speculate how the Shroud might have emerged when and where it did, we nevertheless see a broader context of devotion and artistic patronage from those who knew something about the Shroud in Lirey. The familial association with the baronies in Achaea as we pointed out may be a clue, as Harvard art historian Jeffrey Hamburger noted, that the Shroud, "whatever its origins, derives from Byzantine liturgical cloths of the Epitaphios type."[12]

When unveiled in the Charny collegiate church of Lirey in the fourteenth century, amid English aggression on the surrounding landscape, the Black Death, a schism and papacy in need of legitimizing itself to its constituents, the Shroud resembled the art term *ekphrasis*, the notion of art as a literary device. In this case, the Shroud serves as a mirror to those who gaze upon it. They see not only the Body of Christ, the ultimate relic, but themselves, those who endured so much physical suffering with little hope of escape. Their only escape was by uniting their sorrows with He who subsumed the sins of the world.

---

12 Correspondence with author, January 28, 2020.

PART IV
A SHROUDED JOURNEY

Le siège de Constantinople (1453) by Jean Le Tavernier after 1455

CHAPTER THIRTEEN

FROM FLAX TO TOMB

The Ottoman Turks prepared for their final assault against the Byzantine Empire in the spring of 1453, a pending victory that would signal the dawn of the Ottoman Empire and the renaming of the ancient city of Constantinople to Istanbul. Pope Pius II pleaded at the subsequent Council of Mantua for the Latin west to topple the Islamic power and reassert Christian hegemony. But this was a new era, no longer one of crusade fever that swept Christendom four centuries earlier. Besides, the Latin west had their own unification troubles, marked mainly by the Hundred Years' War.

Among those fallen in battle in that endless war between England and France was the grandfather of one Margaret de Charny, a noblewoman from the family Charny in Burgundy. Geoffroi de Charny was mortally wounded at Poitiers in September 1356, leaving behind a widowed young mother. In turn, his son, Margaret's father, would fall in the wake of a disastrous crusade to Bulgaria some forty years later. Margaret's first husband was another victim of the Hundred Years War, perishing at the famed battle of Agincourt in 1415. When Margaret's second husband died, the childless widow knew she would leave this earth without an offspring to carry on the line of Geoffroi de Charny.

In her possession was what is known today as the Shroud of Turin. The aging Margaret was on a peripatetic mission through the beautiful landscapes of modern-day Belgium and Switzerland armed with the Shroud in her travel baggage and a host of legal issues back home. The canons at the church where the Shroud was stored claimed ownership of it. So did Margaret. When the English were ransacking through Champagne and Burgundy after their success at Agincourt, Margaret and her second husband, Humbert de Villersexel de la Roche, ushered the Shroud to safekeeping to Humbert's estates in the picturesque Doubs Valley near the modern French-Swiss border. A 1418 receipt of the items is preserved indicating this transfer, with the Shroud topping the list. But it never was returned to the canons at Notre-Dame de Lirey, the wooden church Geoffroi de Charny had built a few years before his death.

So vicious was the legal spat that Margaret found herself excommunicated. And in 1453, Marguerite finalized a transfer of the Shroud to new ownership – her kinsmen of the House of Savoy. Like many mysteries around the Shroud, the ambiguity over the exchange leaves many questions. The subsequent history of the Shroud as Savoy property, however, is well attested, but its origins, and, for our purposes, the world in which it emerged, remains unknown to the majority of both the general public and modern-day Roman Catholics.

In 1506, Pope Julius II, Michelangelo's patron and the visionary behind the new Saint Peter's, instituted the Feast of the Holy Shroud for May 4. In 1578, the cardinal of Milan, Saint Charles Borromeo, venerated the cloth in a private showing before participating in an exhibition of the Shroud in Turin before 40,000. Over forty years later, Saint Francis de Sales, bishop of Geneva, held the cloth in an ostension (exhibition) before the people. Copies of the cloth were frequently produced throughout Christendom. King Philip V of Spain's commission for a copy was undertaken by an artist while Mass was being said at the same time mere feet away. In the late seventeenth century, architect Guarino Guarini constructed a special chapel to house the Shroud, the Baroque masterwork Chapel of the Holy Shroud, adjacent to the Turin Cathedral. In 1804, on his way to the coronation of Napoleon, Pope Pius VII venerated the cloth. Eventually, Pius VII would become Napoleon's de facto prisoner in France. Weathering the emperor's tyrannical rule until Napoleon's fall in 1815, Pius returned to Italy, once again visiting the Shroud.

By the end of the nineteenth century, the Shroud's reputation was firmly established as both a holy object and a royal Savoy heirloom. During World War II, as Hitler encouraged occultism within the reich, Christian relics gained Nazi interest. Knowing that desperate times call for desperate measures, the Shroud was secretly ushered out of Turin in 1939 to a location known only to a few – to the Benedictine monastery of Montevergine in central Italy. During a 1943 skirmish with the Americans, Germans occupied the monastery, but the silent monks hovered together in prayer – over the crypt where the Shroud was kept. They were left alone by the soldiers. The Shroud survived one of its many close calls.

After the final collapse of the Savoy monarchy in 1946, the owner of the Shroud, King Umberto II, lived out his remaining decades in exile in Portugal. Upon his death in 1983, the exiled king's will stipulated that the Shroud of Turin, in Savoy possession over 500 years, would now become sole custody of the Roman pontiff.

Still, even after this celebrated history, how did one Marguerite de Charny, with no children or no living immediate family members, even come to own the Shroud?

Even House of Savoy historians differ with competing accounts, some of them clearly attempting to establish a legendary foundation behind the Savoys coming into possession of the Shroud, a literary technique to set a firm *auctoritas*, authority, not only about the subject in question but perhaps more importantly for the author, to give credence to the actual writing. And the Savoys certainly milked the Shroud, so much so it helped catapult them to the heights of power while creating an aura of mystique about the Shroud that only grew with time.

Such a relic ostensibly should have a clear-cut known history, but such is not the case with the Shroud. So foggy is its history before the Savoy era the court's official Shroud historian, Philibertus Pingonius, writing in about 1580, notated two origin stories for the Shroud's journey to the Savoy: as an acquisition after the fall of Constantinople, and that the Savoy obtained it from "a certain illustrious matron," Margaret de Charny, who Pingonius pegs as from the line of Duke Louis's wife, Anne of Cyprus, the long line of Jerusalem kings and queens from the House of Lusignan. This idea was a popular one. Referring to Margaret de Charny as a "princess of Cyprus" was not unusual by historians seeking to explain the Shroud's origins. An 1871 biography of St. Francis de Sales states the Shroud went from Nicodemus to Gamaliel, a character from the Acts of the Apostles, to Saint James the Apostle, and then down through the Lusignan line of royalty until "Princess Margaret," "last of the Lusignan line," brought the Shroud to Chambery. In actuality, the Shroud would not arrive in Chambery until the 1500s. Another account states the Shroud came from Cyprus, the last stronghold of the Latin Kingdom of Jerusalem, and not from Margaret de Charny, the purported Cypriot, but by her grandfather, Geoffroi de Charny himself, who personally obtained the Shroud from the King of Cyprus, and that it was previously in Antioch and Jerusalem. Still another strand tells of the holy shroud under the protection of the bishops of Jerusalem, then the Knights Templar until the order's grand master (Everard des Barres) handed it over to Amadeus III of Savoy. A victim of the Second Crusade, Amadeus died in Cyprus, leaving behind the holy cloth. The kings of Cyprus, of the house of Lusignan, then employed it in military expeditions, including the acquisition of Armenia, suggesting its power as a military battle standard. Following that conquest, somehow Geoffroi de Charny brought it back to France.[1] Such a somewhat obscure connection might be dismissed out of hand until one realizes the Armenian church was deeply devoted to St. Jude Thaddeus, who we will meet later in the legend of King Abgar (or was it another Thaddeus?) and the image of Christ "not made by human hands." There's the enduring thought that the Templars, specifically one Geoffrey de Charney, who was burned at the stake with the last Templar grand master, Jacques de Molay, in 1314, somehow arranged the cloth to be handed off to the family Charny of Cote d'Or, possibly through Jean de Joinville, seneschal of Champagne (the Templar Charney has never been seriously linked with the Charny of Burgundy pedigree).[2] A common hagiographic account tells of Geoffroi de Charny in prison vowing to build a chapel to the Virgin upon his release, where he would place the Shroud given him by the king of Cyprus as earlier as 1330, who procured it after time it spent in Antioch. Entire strands of the Shroud in Germany have ranged from Frederick II Barbarossa procuring the Shroud from Frankish knights to Templars fleeing to Germany and hiding the Shroud in octagonal chapels to a German family buying the title of Charny and bringing the Shroud with them upon emigrating to France. An idea that the heretical Cathars in Languedoc possessed the Shroud, only for it to be snatched by Geoffroi de Charny. A growing thought in today's world of Shroud studies, based on a placard from 1525, is that the Shroud was given to Geoffroi de Charny by Philippe VI of France around 1350.[3] A reasonable claim, except that Geoffroi de Charny was in prison in 1350, Philippe VI died in August 1350, and there is no primary document even suggesting the notion.[4]

The hypotheses are endless,[5] yet the facts that exist say nothing about such a journey for the Shroud. To the Savoy, ultimately, it made no dif-

1 Claude-Antoine Ducis, "Le Saint Suaire a Annecy et La Naissance de Saint Francois de Sales" in *En Revue Savoisienne*, vol. 24, no. 4 (30 April 1883), 33-35.
2 Babinet, however, claims a Templar priest called Milo de Charny is of the same family as Jean de Charny, Geoffroi de Charny's father. Robert Babinet, "'La profession de foi des derniers templiers'" in *La Pensee Catholique* (March/April 1996), 49-74.
3 André-Marie Dubarle and Hilda Leynen, *Histoire ancienne du linceul de Turin*, t. 2, 944–1356 (Paris: François-Xavier de Guibert), 1998.
4 There is, however, an intriguing detail that during Charny's imprisonment, his servant, a William Buynet, was granted safe conduct "until Easter." Thomas Duffus Hardy, *Syllabus of Rymer's Foedera, Vol. 1, 1066-1377* (London: Longmans, Green, & Co., 1869), 368.
5 These continue into our own time, indicative that there is simply no historical record of the Shroud before the end of the fourteenth century. See for instance, Daniel Raffard de Brienne, *Enquete Sur le Saint Suaire* (Paris: Claire Vigne Editrice), 1996; Willi K. Muller, *Festliche Begegungen: Die Freunde des Turiner Grabtuches in zwei Jahrtausenden* (1989); Giovanni Tucci, "I De Toucy e la Custodia della sindone Geoffroy de Charny e Guillaume de Toucy" in Nicolaus Studi Storici, vol. 9, no. 2 (1998), 647-664; and the Q manuscript in Bruxelles folio 9630 that apparently mentions a shroud in Troyes. See J-P Martin, "Notes sur le ms. de Bruxelles de Garin le Lorrain," 319-326.

ference how it got to Duke Louis I of Savoy and his wife, Princess Anne sometime in 1453. The mystique created around it, from the Baroque architecture of the Holy Shroud Chapel to the cloth's infrequent expositions, only enhanced when photographs of the Shroud circled the globe in 1898.

Each of the four canonical Gospels and the apocryphal Gospel of Peter cite the role of Joseph of Arimathea as instrumental in procuring the burial cloth to quickly wrap the body of Jesus of Nazareth before sundown.[6] But Joseph of Arimathea is a mysterious figure, and the Gospels contradict each other on who exactly he is. "According to Matthew and John, Joseph was a disciple of Jesus, but Mark and Luke say that he was a member of the Sanhedrin, while Peter says that he was a friend of both Jesus and Pilate."[7] What they do agree on, however, is that this Joseph took charge of burying Christ, even as they elide the minutiae of the burial itself.

What the Gospels do not state is how exactly Joseph purchased the Shroud. Perhaps a vendor at the bazaar near the Damascus Gate, looking to make final purchases before closing for Passover? Or was it custom prepared, the loyal member of the Sanhedrin anticipating the future crucifixion of his savior as He prophesied?

It is true, first millennium accounts speak of a burial cloth retained in Jerusalem in the centuries after the Resurrection. A Frankish bishop named Arculf on his pilgrimage to the Holy Land observed the purported burial cloth of Christ and even measured it, deeming it to be eight feet. Those who favor that what we know as the Shroud of Turin was really the Image of Edessa, however, dismiss this "Arculf shroud" since their shroud, the true shroud of Christ, was in modern-day Turkey at this time. At some point, at least according to Heinrich Joseph Floss, the "sudarium" of the Lord was ushered out of Jerusalem to Constantinople for fear of the Moslems.

We see, then, that the very linen itself is a point of contention in the Shroud debate.

Linen is a textile made from cultivated flax plants. Linen fibers are harvested from the plant to produce various textiles. The Bible references linen as early as Genesis and always as an element in a special – if not royal – occasion. "Then Pharaoh took off his signet ring from his hand and put it on Joseph's hand, and clothed him in garments of fine linen and put the

---

6 Cf. Jn 19:38-42; Mk 15:45-46; Lk 23:53; Mt 27:59-60; Gospel of Peter, 23-24
7 Andrea Nicolotti, "An Ignominious Burial: The Treatment of the Body of Jesus of Nazareth" in *Public Uses of Human Remains and Relics in History*, ed. S. Cavicchioli and L. Provero (New York: Routledge, 2020), 11-28.

gold necklace around his neck,"[8] revealing Egypt's use of linen. Indeed, the climate of the Middle East is conducive to the cultivation of the flax plants.

Dr. Orit Shamir of the Israel Antiquities Authority in Jerusalem opined the Shroud of Turin was not produced in the Land of Israel.[9] Shamir's study focused on the Shroud's weaving technique. As can be seen in close-up study today, the Shroud was woven in a herringbone weave in a 3:1 twill, meaning three warp (vertical) threads for every single weft (horizontal) thread. In other words, the Shroud of Turin was neither flimsy nor cheap. In this way, it corresponded with the fine linen purchased by Joseph of Arimathea.

It was precisely because of this weaving technique, however, that Dr. Shamir concluded the Shroud "was probably not manufactured in the Land of Israel neither in the Roman nor in the Medieval period."[10] In Shamir's analysis, no textiles fashioned in the manner of the Shroud have been found in the Land of Israel. Thus, he suggested, the Shroud was of European creation from the Middle Ages when such patterns were more commonplace. Given the prominence of textile production in Flanders, for instance, or exchange at the Champagne Trade Fairs near where Geoffroi de Charny's Lirey chapel was located, there were any number of locales in which a medieval linen shroud could have been produced.

In Paolo Aringhi's work from the 17th century, *Roma Subterranea Novissima*, Aringhi cited a passage from Vergil's *Aeneid*, when Pallas, the young son of King Evander, is killed in battle. The youth is laid on a funeral pyre and Aeneas brings forth an expensive purple and gold embroidered cloth, woven by the very hands of "*Sidonia Dido*," referring to Dido, the Queen of Carthage. The adjective modifying Dido, "Sidonia," is used elsewhere in Vergil meaning something like luxurious.

When Anghri speaks of the linen cloth covering Christ, he builds off his citation of Vergil's "Sidonia Dido" by referencing Tyre and Sidon, the coastal cities north of Galilee in modern-day Lebanon. They were Phoenician towns. In Alex Johnston Warden's book, *The Linen Trade*, Warden wrote of linen as crucial not only in Phoenician trade with Egyptians, but

---

8   Gen. 41:42
9   Orit Shamir, "A Burial Textile from the First Century CE in Jerusalem Compared to Roman Textiles in the Land of Israel and the Turin Shroud," SHS Web Conferences 15, no. 10 (2015). Also Andrea Nicolotti, "La Sindone di Torino in quanto tessuto: analisi storica, tecnica, comparativa" in *Non solum circulatorum ludo similia: Miscellanea di studi sul Cristianesimo del primo millennio*, ed. Valerio Polidori (Rome: Amazon KDP, 2018), 148-204.
10 Shamir, 8, 10.

in canvas for their sails,[11] since Phoenicians were expert navigators, just as Herodotus attested.[12] Herodotus also famously details an Egyptian embalming process where bandages of fine linen are cut into strips.[13]

It was in Tyre and Sidon where dyes were employed, centers of producing expensive purple linen. Warden also affirms linen's ultimate role in salvation history: "The last mention of linen in the Bible is in reference to the glorious hereafter – to the heavenly Jerusalem."[14]

S-twist and Z-twist are two ways fabric is spun:

Courtesy Andrea Nicolotti

As Shamir and others have noted, "textiles in wool and linen from parts of the Eastern Roman provinces, such as Syria and Palestine, show a preference for S-twisted yarns."[15] Textiles expert Lise Bender Jørgensen went on to note, on the other hand, "In the northern Roman provinces and much of Europe, Z-twisted yarn was the norm since c. 500 BC and throughout the first millennium AD."[16] The Shroud is Z-twist.[17]

11 Alex Johnson Warden, *The Linen Trade* (London: Roberts and Green, 1864), 176-180.
12 Herodotus, *The Histories*, trans. George Rawlinson (New York: Dutton & Co., 1862), 1.2.
13 Ibid., 2.86.
14 Warden, 143.
15 Lise Bender Jørgensen, "Textiles and Textiles Trade in the First Millennium AD," in *Trade in the Ancient Sahara and Beyond*, ed. D. Mattingly et al. (Cambridge: Cambridge UP, 2017), 238.
16 Ibid.
17 Nicolotti, 153-154.

Artist rendering by Paul Vignon, *Le Saint Suaire De Turin Devant La Science, L'Archeologie, L'Histoire, L'Iconographie, La Logique*, 1938

CHAPTER FOURTEEN

POSITIVES AND NEGATIVES

In its first centuries when the Church was outlawed and persecuted, a practice of preserving the most intimate truths, or "secrets" of the faith from being known to non-Christians in order to safeguard the faith, was common. Such a custom is today referred to as the "discipline of the secrets." As the Aristotelian maxim goes, *Quod ille majestatem minuit secretorum, qui secreta indignis divulgat;*[1] "The one who divulges secrets to the unworthy lessens the majesty of mysteries."[2]

A "secret" was revealed to amateur photographer and professional lawyer Secondo Pia on the night of May 26, 1898 in Turin. It became the photograph seen around the world, and one that singlehandedly ushered the Shroud onto the global stage of attention while inviting newfound curiosity and a wave of scientific speculation upon it throughout the twentieth century.

A self-taught photographer, Pia gained a bit of a reputation in the Piedmont region of Italy for his photography, earning a gold medal at the inaugural Italian Architectural Exposition in 1890. At the time, Italy was officially unified for two decades, and in 1898 Italy's King Umberto I of the Royal House of Savoy sought to hold a celebration. His vision was twofold: to celebrate the 50th anniversary of the Constitution of Sardinia, the Statuto, which formed the legal groundwork for the Kingdom of Italy, and to mark the 400th anniversary of the completion of Turin's cathedral, Saint John the Baptist.

What especially interested the organizers of the festivities was an exhibition of the House of Savoy's prized relic, retained in the Turin Cathedral since 1578 – the Shroud of Turin. Well known throughout European Christendom by its propaganda machine, the House of Savoy succeeded in establishing an aura and mystique around the relic. Only on a few occasions – six times in the nineteenth century alone – was the Shroud publicly displayed, typically for Savoy family celebrations, such as the wedding of King Umberto's parents, Victor Emmanuel and Adelaide of Austria, in 1842.

While King Umberto approved of the Shroud's exhibit for May 1898, he was less inclined to something else the planners encouraged: to allow

---

1   Edwin Greenlaw, "Some Old Religious Cults in Spenser," in *Studies in Philology, Vol. 20* (Chapel Hill: UNC Press, 1923), 224, n30.
2   Ibid., 224.

for the Shroud to be photographed for the first time. The relatively new invention of photography was both gradually taking the world by storm and yet still in its infancy, with camera equipment clunky, cumbersome, and often unreliable. Simply, the Catholic king wondered if it was not sacrilegious for the enormous equipment to be brought into the cathedral and to expose the relic for the sake of a camera lens.

Barron Manno, a trusted adviser to the king, urged that the Shroud be photographed. It was Manno who identified the Secondo Pia as the official photographer tasked with capturing the Shroud of Turin on film for the first time. Finally, a month from the planned dates of the public exhibition, the king acquiesced. The Shroud could be photographed. For this opportunity, Pia offered to cover all equipment costs himself and surrendered claims to copyright.

The Shroud was to be exhibited inside the Turin cathedral from May 25 to June 2, 1898. Pia's first opportunity to photograph the wholly exposed cloth as a trial test was scheduled for the night of May 25, during a temporary closure of the cathedral and with impatient pilgrims hovering outside.

Pia faced challenges from the outset. The photographer had never even personally witnessed the cloth, for one. The last time it was exhibited was 1868, when Pia was thirteen years old. Of those who witnessed the Shroud then, incidentally, was Saint John Bosco and his pupils. Additionally, cathedral lighting was not nearly enough for photography purposes. Pia thus had to rely on electric lightbulbs, considered the first time such bulbs were employed in photography. Pia was also at the mercy of the exhibition hours. Anyone familiar with the task of capturing live events for media purposes knows the real world does not easily accommodate the requirements of cameras. Rather than meeting Pia's technical needs, the focus was on keeping the hordes of pilgrims moving, not unlike those at the Metropolitan Cathedral-Basilica today who gaze upon the tilma of Our Lady of Guadalupe while on a tract.

Pia's attempts on May 25 were underexposed. The diffusion glass in front of his lights broke as he tried to get uniform lighting on the whole of the 14-foot, 5-inch by 3-foot, 7 inches linen cloth. Pia's next opportunity, and his last, was at 9:30 the night of Saturday, May 28. Aided by photography enthusiasts Don Nogier de Malijay, Don Solano, and Lt. Felice Fino, Pia encountered a whole new problem. "A crystal [had] been placed in front of the Holy Shroud to protect it from dust and that made my work more difficult," Pia later noted in a 1907 letter to Arthur Loth.

But this time Pia was determined to complete his work. After rigging the tripods, lights, and diffusion, Pia exposed two 50x60 centimeter plates using a Voigtlander lens (still on the market today), with a faint yellow filter. The first exposure length was fourteen minutes and the second twenty minutes. Immediately afterwards, the team retired to Pia's dark room. What followed is forever steeped in Shroud lore: In Pia's dark room was the revelation of a long-kept "discipline of the secret" the Shroud held until this moment.

Pia stared wordlessly at the haunting but peaceful face of the man in repose. He was convinced, he later related, that he was staring at the crucified Jesus of Nazareth.

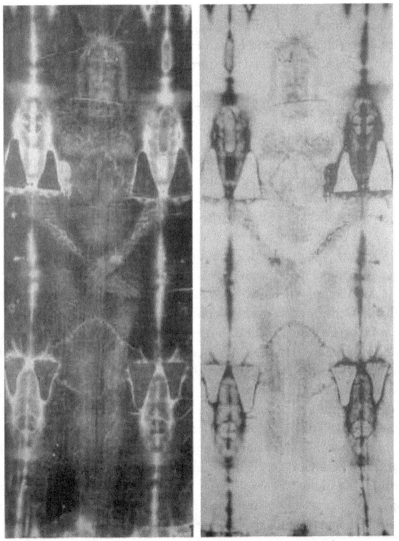

The Shroud of Turin in both negative and positive photographic formats.

This moment of discovery, as night turned into morning in the spring of 1898, a week after Ascension Thursday, was a moment of profound faith for Secondo Pia. It is also often cited as the inciting incident when, by way of the Shroud, religious faith and modern science met.

Pia's photographs were secretly sent to the king, but by mid-June they were splashed across two Italian dailies, and were featured in the Vatican's *L'Osservatore Romano* on June 15. The Shroud leaped overnight from the forgotten pages of history into the popular culture stratosphere as journals and periodicals ruminated on the image, reviewed the known history of the Shroud, and sought to explain how such an image appeared on a ragged cloth. "The photograph is stupendously successful and has an exceptional importance for religion history and science," raved the *Corrierre Nazionale* on June 14.

Not everyone championed Secondo Pia's photographs as a miraculous discovery. Among these was the formidable researcher-cleric, canon Ulysse Chevalier. In light of Pia's photograph and the subsequent popularity spike of Shroud interest, Chevalier set his own mammoth medieval bibliographic research aside and devoted a response to Pia and the supporters who found in the photograph the face of Jesus Christ. Chevalier saw only historical evidence for a medieval creation. Chevalier followed up his first work on the Shroud with another in 1902, *Le Saint Suaire de Lirey-Chambéry, Turin et les défenseurs de son authenticité*, which includes a number of original documents. It was a response to the hypotheses of Paul Vignon.

Paul Vignon (1865-1943) was something of a wandering soul when the controversy over Pia's photographs and the debate about the Shroud's true nature reached a fever pitch. He was born in Lyon, the same city where Ulyssee Chevalier taught history at the Catholic Institute. Originally pursuing the study of biology, and while he would eventually become a professor of zoology and biology in Paris later in life, Vignon's penchant as a Renaissance Man conflicted with the daily practical demands of the contemporary world. He found Alpine climbing a way to work out his thoughts, and as a practicing Catholic, to hear where God was calling him. Jesuit Paul De Gail wrote of Vignon, "As a biologist enraptured by the enigmas of nature, as a philosopher of very acute sensibility, as a man of deep religious faith, he rejoiced whenever, in his quests, spiritual explanations were revealed."[3]

---

3   Paul De Gail, "Paul Vignon," https://www.shroud.com/pdfs/ssi06part7.pdf.

On one of his expeditions scaling the Alps, Vignon met a fellow-traveler, a Catholic priest named Achille Ratti, named after Achilles, the great mythological hero of the Trojan War. Vignon and Achille Ratti joined forces on one particular climb, sharing personal thoughts on God and the world as such occasions provide.

At the age of thirty, the energetic but wayward Vignon suffered a nervous breakdown. Convalescing in Switzerland, Vignon found comfort in painting, and like most everything else he attempted, he discovered he had some talent for the art. His science background fused with his artistic interest would later be fulfilled in his passion for the Shroud of Turin.

Vignon's mentor, Sorbonne professor of zoology Yves Delage, offered Vignon a job at the magazine Delage was the founder and editor, *The Biological Year*. Here Vignon, now about 35, seemed to hit his stride. But when Delage showed Vignon the Secondo Pia negative photograph of the face on the Shroud, Vignon was hooked. And so was the agnostic Delage – despite having no affiliation with Christianity. Vignon was thrilled when Delage sent him on an investigative mission: to meet Secondo Pia directly, and determine what lay behind the mysterious image on the linen cloth.

Pia warmly received Vignon in Turin and walked him through his photographic process. While somewhat versed in the art of painting, in truth Vignon knew next to nothing about photography at the time. Yet he kept his composure, and Pia was encouraged enough that he passed on copies of his Shroud photos to Vignon. Also during the encounter, Vignon interviewed those who accompanied Pia in the cathedral for the photography sessions in May 1898. Vignon became convinced this was no mere forgery – neither by Pia nor likely in the origins of the image itself.

At the Sorbonne Vignon and Delage mulled over the logical ways in which the dual imprint was achieved on the cloth. Both worked from the basis of the crucifixion. In Vignon's book on the Shroud he would publish in 1902, *The Shroud of Christ*, the book's frontispiece includes a reproduction of Giulio Clovio's Renaissance painting featuring angels, surrounded by cherub, displaying the Shroud in its vertical position, while below Joseph of Arimathea, Nicodemus, and the disciple John wrap the linen cloth over the crucified Jesus at the foot of the cross in the way it appeared to be wrapped on the man on the Shroud.

Giulio Clovio (1498-1578)

Vignon's biological background and Delage's anatomical skillset meshed well, supplemented with assistance by René Colson, Assistant Professor of Physics at the École Polytechnique; Armand Gautier, Professor of Biological Medicine; and journalists J. de Gaux and Arthur Loth. The scientists developed a series of arguments based on the Pia photographs. The full body image of the man was shockingly realistic, they admitted, well beyond anything an artist could have achieved. The anatomy was accurate. From his years studying painting Vignon could not detect any school of artistic influence on the image. The dark brown stains populating the cloth were so convincing as bloodstains they must have been real. It appeared the body's core, particularly the back and lower half, was entirely riddled with wounds. The explosive bloodstain at the wrist and in the chest continually haunted Vignon over the course of his study of the Shroud. Again and again it felt as if he was peering down at a visual Gospel.

The biggest challenge for the group was identifying how certain body parts registered more intensely on the cloth than others. One experiment even involved a willing volunteer – Vignon – who was doused in powder before a sheet soaked in albumen (the protein from egg white) covered him. These inventive tests proved fruitless.

It was Colson who finally put forward a new thought, based on a line of research he conducted a few years earlier: he discovered powder from zinc gives off vapors in a dark environment, which a photographic plate would detect. It was an idea far more promising than anything suggested to that point. But how would that work in the case of the Shroud?

Another slew of experiments ensued with medallions and sculptures. Colson was right, the zinc powder did vaporize onto the cloth, but nowhere near the uniform precision found on the Shroud's image. Colson then remembered the special anointing recipe from the Pentateuch:

> The LORD told Moses: Take the finest spices: five hundred shekels of free-flowing myrrh; half that amount, that is, two hundred and fifty shekels, of fragrant cinnamon; two hundred and fifty shekels of fragrant cane; five hundred shekels of cassia – all according to the standard of the sanctuary shekel; together with a hin of olive oil; and blend them into sacred anointing oil, perfumed ointment expertly prepared. With this sacred anointing oil you shall anoint the tent of meeting and the Ark of the Covenant...[4]

The idea was then put forward: what if the cloth, not the body, was covered with the spices? Gautier, the professor of biological medicine, took the concept a step further. Given the state of the body on the cloth – someone who was clearly a victim of torture, dripping in both blood and sweat, not to mention whatever natural elements the body collected – alkaline vapors would likely be emitted, as opposed to the acidic vapors given off by one who dies a natural death.

---

4 Ex 30:22-26

A further test was then conducted, utilizing Gautier's alkaline chemical. A plaster hand dipped in ammonia was covered by a suede glove. This was then exposed to a cloth soaked in the spices based on the Exodus anointing recipe. Indeed, while again not as uniformly perfect as the image on the linen Shroud, the team agreed their experimentation was enough to put forward a rational explanation for image formation.

Vignon summarized it succinctly: he and his colleagues believed the stained imprint of the man on the Shroud was created not simply by contact, but from a vapograph process. Vignon borrowed a phrase from physics to clarify this thought – "action at a distance," meaning, according to Vignon, that between the sweat and burial spices, the image "diffused" onto the cloth over a period of time. While not completely satisfied with this concept, and indeed one that would be discarded over time, it nevertheless served its purpose for the team at the time.

Meanwhile, Yves Delage was busy turning heads at the French Academy of Science, the venerable institution founded in 1666 by the Sun King, Louis XIV. Delage was a member of the academy, and a respected one at that. His lucid views on science and reason, unfiltered by influence such as religion, made him well liked. He and his colleagues, after all, were products of a post-revolution France, all coming of age during the anti-clerical era of the French Third Republic, the form of government that would last up to the moment the Nazis marched into France in 1940.

And so Delage was met with not a little incredulity and downright embarrassment when he proposed to deliver a lecture before his scientific colleagues of the academy, based on the findings Vignon published in April 1902, *The Shroud of Christ*. Academy members were nonplussed. The 75-year-old academy secretary and renowned chemist, Marcellin Berthelot, was most opposed. The atheist had spent a lifetime decrying the Church in France, his opinions long publicized, and he wanted nothing more than to vanquish "the poisonous vapours of superstition" from the public discourse. Thus, for Berthelot, it went without saying that the Shroud of Turin did not remotely qualify to be discussed in the academy halls.

But Delage remained calm, and his reasoned appeal to the academy board coupled with his stellar reputation prevailed. He would be allowed to deliver the lecture.

On Monday, April 21, 1902, nearly four years after Secondo Pia's photography sessions of the Shroud, the hall at the Institut de France, less than a mile from the Sainte-Chapelle and Notre-Dame, filled in a buzz of nervous anticipation. Berthelot was of course front and center. Arthur Loth, an Academy member, was in attendance. Vignon receded anonymously into a balcony corner. De Gaux was covering it for *L'Univers et le Monde*. But this was Delage's hour. He was staking his entire professional reputation on this lecture.

For a half hour Delage clinically gave an overview of the Shroud properties, its known history from its emergence in the public sphere in the fourteenth century, and a recounting of the tests his team conducted. This is not a painting, Delage stated. Science had shown that. It also showed the cloth's image was not consciously manipulated or forged by other means. It was science, Delage continued, that provided the window into the image formation.

Delage went on. "Add to this, that in order for the image to have formed itself without being ultimately destroyed, it was necessary that the corpse remain in the Shroud at least twenty-four hours, the amount of time needed for the formation of the image, and at most several days, after which putrefaction sets in, which destroys the image and finally the Shroud."[5]

"Tradition – more or less apocryphal, I would say – tells us that this is precisely what happened to Christ; dead on Friday and," Delage paused ever so slightly, "disappeared on Sunday." Then he said it. "The man on the Shroud was the Christ."

Delage's lecture also included Pia's photographs posted on a blackboard for the audience to view. Journalist Horace Blanchon, whose article on the lecture would appear two days later in *Figaro*, confessed, "I have here before me, since an hour ago, two photographic images, exhibited at the Academy of Sciences by Monsieur Yves Delage, Professor of Zoology at the Sorbonne. By tomorrow, their story will have gone around the world, for they are the most mysterious, the most improbable, and the most impressive pictures that one could possibly imagine. How can I tell," he continued, "how can I express to others the emotion they arouse in me?"

The title of Delage's paper was "Imprints produced on a sheet by emanations from a corpse." Standard practice for papers delivered at the Academy was they would appear in the journal *Comptes rendus*. But Berthelot informed Delage on the night of April 21 all references to Christ and the Shroud would be excised, and the paper instead retitled, "Chemistry: On the formation of negative images by the action of certain vapors." Such is how it appears in the *Comptes rendus* to this day. It was the first blow to Delage.

---

5 Quoted in Picknett and Prince, *Turin Shroud: In Whose Image?* (Harper Collins: New York, 1994), 157.

A review of the lecture in the May 24, 1902 issue of *Scientific American* quoted Jesuit Herbert Thurston, who pointed to Ulysse Chevalier's writings favoring the Shroud as a medieval fabrication, and the Jesuit periodical *Analecta Bollandiana* stated Chevalier's word was final. The review concluded by pointing out the number of extant cloths claimed to be the true shroud that wrapped the crucified Christ, and the Turin cloth being just one of them.

Other journal articles, such as in *Revue Scientifique*, employed phrases such as "intellectual ineptitude" and "conspiracy" in critiquing Delage and Vignon's findings, and using ad hominem attacks on Delage, Vignon and their colleagues as "seminarians disguised as scientists."

Delage himself responded in a letter at the end of May, and it would prove to be his last public statement on his work on the Shroud of Turin. "[It has been said that] I have betrayed science and have not been true to my convictions as a free-thinker. For these persons, I want to reestablish the facts." Citing how much of his paper was left out of the official lecture publication, Delage recounted the salient points. He continued:

> I have been faithful to the true scientific spirit, treating this argument with the sole intention to find the truth, without worrying whether I have served the interests of this or that other religious sector. Those, instead, who allowed themselves to be influenced by such concerns are the ones who have betrayed the scientific method. I have not made a clerical work, because clericalism and anticlericalism have nothing to do in this affair. I consider the Christ to be an historical personage and I do not see why anyone should be scandalised that there exists a material trace of his existence.[6]

Yves Delage died in 1920 at age 66. For the last eight years of his life, he worked in total blindness, but still edited *The Biological Year*. In the wake of the press from the lecture, Secondo Pia remained ostracized in Turin, still under suspicion for forging his infamous images. His 1907 letter to Arthur Loth was his attempt to preserve the historical record amid scandal.

In 1931, commemorating the marriage of Prince Umberto II of Savoy and Princess Marie José of Belgium, the Shroud would again be exposed for the first time since 1898. Between 1.5 and 2 million pilgrims passed before the Shroud. Photographer Giuseppe Enrie, armed with the most state of the art photographic equipment available, was commissioned by the royal house to photograph the Shroud.

---

6 Yves Delage, Letter to Charles Richet, May 1902.

And just like Pia in 1898, Enrie had access at night after the exhibit closed to photograph the Shroud, brought out from its location in the Guarini chapel into the cathedral itself. Accompanying Enrie and his team on the night of May 22 in the cathedral was none other than Paul Vignon, now 65. For three decades now Vignon was silent on the Shroud of Turin, much like his mentor, Yves Delage. But the new exhibition aroused in him his old passion for the linen cloth – and the image on it.

In Enrie's final photography session on the night of May 23, another name from the past returned to witness Enrie in action. 76-year-old Secondo Pia observed the proceedings in quiet dignity, 34 years after his own photos made him the subject of ridicule and accusations. He was flanked by interested members from the French Academy of Science.

Emphasizing details and contrast, Enrie exposed twelve orthochromatic plates, including a life-size image and seven-time enlargement of the wrist wound. Enrie, as Pia before him, did no post-production touchups. The pristine black-and-white prints became the most well known images of the Shroud for most of the twentieth century. And just as Pia found in 1898, Enrie confirmed by his photo negatives that indeed the negative was in fact a positive image of the man on the Shroud. Secondo Pia died in Turin in 1941, at final peace that his photography opened a new door into the study of the Shroud.

In the fall of 1933 and at the request of the current pope, Pius XI, the Shroud was again exhibited for three weeks as part of the Holy Year jubilee marking two millennia of the Redemption. Paul Vignon, elated by the astonished responses of Giuseppe Enrie's photos, was one of the few scientists permitted to examine the Shroud up close for one night. The experience was the basis for his second book on the Shroud following *The Shroud of Christ* from 1902, which he published in 1938 – *The Holy Shroud of Turin: Science, Archaeology, History, Iconography, Logic.* For this effort, Vignon was awarded a prize – by none other than the French Academy of Science.

The 1933 exhibition, the last major public exhibition of the Shroud for forty-five years, was only made possible by the intent of the Roman pontiff, Pius XI. After all, Pope Pius had long harbored a personal interest in the Shroud, having attended the 1898 exhibition as a young man of 32. He also had a personal connection with one of the scientists who devoted so much to introducing the Shroud to the modern world – Paul Vignon, his old buddy from Alpine climbing days. Pius XI was Achille Ratti.

Exhibition of the Shroud, 1933.

Chapter Fifteen

Modern Times

The explosive interest of the Shroud at the turn of the twentieth century identified two distinct camps: those who favored authenticity, and those who decidedly did not. Such a divide continues into our own time. The study of the Shroud is a veritable booming industry. In our own century, education offerings such as the Postgraduate Certificate in Shroud Studies at the Science and Faith Institute of the Pontifical Athenaeum *Regina Apostolorum* have increased. Shroud centers populate the globe, and the photographic negative image has been used on holy cards.

A great part of the Shroud's mystique is owed to its rare public appearances. In recent history, it was exhibited in 1998 and during the Great Jubilee of 2000. It was shown again in 2010, 2015, and exposed for livestreaming purposes on Holy Saturday 2020, during the unprecedented lockdown due to the novel coronavirus pandemic.[1] The 1988 Carbon-14 test done by labs at the University of Arizona, University of Oxford, and University of Zurich[2] proved only a temporary roadblock in the quest to authenticate the Shroud as the first century Palestinian burial cloth of Jesus. In tandem with this pursuit, hypotheses of how the image of the figure appeared on the cloth increasingly point to the event of the resurrection.

No formal testing of the cloth itself has been sanctioned by the Holy See and Archdiocese of Turin or performed on the Shroud since the 1988 C-14 test. Thus, the dating tests that seek to overturn the medieval findings of the Carbon dating test are ultimately only speculative, until another formal investigation is opened. That sindonologists are behind the testing limits the veracity of their findings to those who wish the Shroud to be the actual cloth of Christ. It is a matter of choosing to believe what one wants to believe, despite the discrepancies for authenticity shown by

---

1 In a letter to Turin archbishop Nosiglia regarding the special event, Pope Francis wrote, "In the face of the Man of the Shroud we also see the faces of many sick brothers and sisters, especially those who are more lonely and less cared for; but also all the victims of wars and violence, slavery and persecution." Edward Pentin, "Coronavirus Latest from Rome," *National Catholic Register*, 9 April 2020, https://www.ncregister.com/blog/edward-pentin/coronavirus-latest-italys-bishops-call-for-all-churches-to-be-closed.

2 "Radiocarbon Dating of the Shroud of Turin" in *Nature*, Vol. 337, No. 6208 (16 February 1989), 611-615.

the 1988 C-14 test and the lack of the Shroud as we know it detailed in the historical record.[3]

It is beyond the scope of this work to detail the debates about the C-14 findings, for instance, the belief by the late thermochemist Dr. Ray Rogers, who personally examined the Shroud: "[T]he radiocarbon sample had been dyed. Specifically, the color and distribution of the coating implies that repairs were made at an unknown time with foreign linen dyed to match the older original material." Therefore, Rogers summarized, "The radiocarbon sample was thus not part of the original cloth and is invalid for determining the age of the shroud."[4] University of Padua professor of mechanical and thermal measurements Dr. Giulio Fanti carried out multiple studies on fibers from the Shroud procured from Dr. Giovanni Riggi, the man charged to cut the corner sample in 1988. Essentially, Fanti averaged his results and determined an origin date of the Shroud as between 283 B.C. and A.D. 217.

On the other hand, at a 2014 meeting of the American Academy of Forensic Sciences, Dr. Matteo Borrini and Luigi Garlaschelli presented their paper, "A BPA Approach to the Shroud of Turin," which was later published in the January 2019 issue of *Journal of Forensic Sciences*. Using a living volunteer, the investigation studied the blood pattern formations on the Shroud's image. The paper concluded that the bloodstains visible on the Shroud were unrealistic to a corpse that had been crucified and subsequently buried.

Meanwhile, Fanti turned his research from the age of the cloth to the image on the Shroud. Fanti worked with a team and sculptor Sergio Rodella on the creation of a life-size plaster statue based on the specifications of the image – replete with facial accuracy, wound marks, and blood flows. Their goal was to better understand the configuration of how the cloth was wrapped, and perhaps shed some light on the mysterious image formation.

La Stampa's "Vatican Insider" noted the statue revealed that the man on the Shroud "was not in supine position, but, due to rigor mortis, his bust is rotated, his head bowed and knees bent. His dislocated shoulders, already documented for some time, explain how it was possible to join the arms of the corpse to cover the pubis without them being tied."[5]

3 Professor of History of the Crusades at the University of Oxford, Christopher Tyerman, for example, was quite frank in describing the Shroud as a medieval forgery from the fourteenth century. Correspondence with author, November 11, 2018.
4 Raymond N. Rogers, "Studies on the radiocarbon dating of the Shroud of Turin" in *Thermochimica Acta*, Volume 425, Issue 1-2 (January 2005), 189-194.
5 Andrea Cionci, "Shroud, here is the 3D reconstruction of the wrapped body" in *Vatican Insider in English*, 6 April 2018, https://www.lastampa.it/vatican-insider/en/2018/04/06/news/shroud-

Fanti also found the figure on the Shroud's right shoulder was severely dislocated. The model also is depicted with his chin towards his neck, and his knees bent, again based on the position of the image on the Shroud. We will see in the next chapter how closely this model corresponds with similar effigies of Christ in the tomb (or on a stone slab, the Stone of Unction) from the fourteenth century. In many ways, the University of Padua's 3D life-size representation completes what U.S. Air Force Academy professors and students attempted in the mid-late 1970s. They determined the frontal image on the cloth was that of a 5-foot-10-inch man. Fanti's model was closer to 5'11".

Professor John Jackson was the physicist at the Air Force Academy who led that particular model reconstruction. Teamed with colleague Eric Jumper, their work coincided at the time with studies by NASA Jet Propulsion Laboratory's Donald Lynn and Jean Lorre. Alerted to the uniqueness of the cloth by members of the Holy Shroud Guild in New York, Lynn and Lorre employed NASA's image processing techniques. While they could not conclude how the image was produced, Lynn and Lorre were certain the image was not hand-painted. Meanwhile, Jackson, Jumper, and Pete Schumacher conducted an analysis of a photograph of the Shroud using a VP8 Image Analyzer, and found that the image on the photograph had three dimensional properties.[6] Such a phenomenon is not totally unknown in photography, but it certainly added more layers to the Shroud mystique. Like most who gaze upon the Shroud, the researchers were hooked. Jackson and Jumper led a team of Americans in an unprecedented examination of the Shroud in 1978 dubbed the Shroud of Turin Research Project (STURP), sponsored by the Holy Shroud Guild.

Yet despite these intensive analyses, the formation of the image could still not be explained. John Jackson did not rule out the possibility of some kind of radiation energy capable of producing a perfect three-dimensional negative image, namely, "by an intense burst of vacuum ultraviolet radiation produced a discoloration on the uppermost surface of the Shroud's fibrils (without scorching it)."[7] This concept is now commonly promoted in many Catholic presentations and publications as the true reason for the impression of the man on the cloths – in other words, jargon for the Resurrection.

---

here-is-the-3d-reconstruction-of-the-wrapped-body-1.34001481.

6 See "How Image Enhancement May Explain Past Events" in JPL Universe, July 5, 1977, https://er.jsc.nasa.gov/seh/shroud.html.

7 Magis Center, "How Did the Shroud of Turin Get Its Image? (Hint: think radiation.)" May 27, 2019, https://magiscenter.com/how-did-shroud-turin-get-image/. See also Paolo Di Lazzaro, "Shroud-like coloration of linen by ultraviolet radiation" given at Incontro Centri di Sindonologia per la festa liturgica della S. Sindone, 2 May 2015, https://www.shroud.com/pdfs/duemaggioDiLazza-roENG.pdf.

But these are not the only hypotheses posited in recent years about the Shroud. Advancing the late Dr. Alan Whanger's belief that a Roman lepton coin can be seen on an eye of the figure on the Shroud,[8] not unlike Barbara Frale claiming to find writing that appeared to be a death certificate for Jesus of Nazareth,[9] a technique called photogrammetric restitution was employed on photographs of the image by an institute in Palermo, Italy (International Institute for Advanced Studies of Space Representation Sciences) that claimed the Crown of Thorns was made out of a branch from Sarcopoterium spinosum, a genus in the rose family. Additionally, the same study identified a tefillah on the figure on the cloth, from a Jewish prayer custom where one tefillin is tied around the left arm, and the other around the head, with a small box containing biblical scrolls, something Alan Whanger also claimed to have discovered via a process he dubbed the "Polarized Image Overlay Technique."[10]

Meanwhile, and on the other hand, other publications argued how the image might be created in the medieval period. Emily A. Craig and Randall R. Bresee argued for the carbon dust drawing technique as a means to produce the image on the cloth.[11] N.D. Wilson suggested only painted glass and sunlight was needed for the image to be created.[12] Professor Nicholas PL Allen focused on early photographic techniques, such as the *camera obscura*, which he argues may have been implemented by a fourteenth century artist.[13]

Meaning "dark chamber," *camera obscura* "and [its] earliest versions, dating to antiquity, consisted of small darkened rooms with light admitted through a single tiny hole. The result was that an inverted image of the outside scene was cast on the opposite wall, which was usually whitened. For centuries the technique was used for viewing eclipses of the Sun without endangering the eyes."[14] The method was employed by Vermeer during the Dutch Baroque period of the 17th century, a

8 John C. Iannone, *The Three Cloths of Christ: The Emerging Treasures of Christianity* (Kissimmee, FL: NorthStar Productions, LLC and Lulu Press, 2009), 45-49.

9 Mark Memmott, "'Death Certificate' Could Be Sign 'Shroud of Turin' is Real, Researcher Says," NPR, November 20, 2009, https://www.npr.org/sections/thetwo-way/2009/11/death_certificate_could_be_sig.html.

10 Spacereinstitute, "The new astonishing phenomenon detected on the Shroud," YouTube video, October 6, 2019, https://www.youtube.com/watch?v=PNUNcJHfKvQ. See also Iannone, 19.

11 Emily A. Craig and Randall R. Bresee, "Image Formation on the Shroud of Turin" in *Journal of Imaging Science and Technology*, Vol. 34, No. 1, 1994.

12 N.D. Wilson, "Father Brown Fakes the Shroud," *Christianity Today*: Books and Culture, March/April 2005.

13 Nicholas PL Allen, "An Overview of the Photographic Hypothesis for Image Formation as it Applies to the Shroud of Lirey-Chambéry-Turin" in Approfondimento Sindone, Anno II, Vol.1, 1998, 25-42.

14 "Camera obscura" in *Encyclopedia Brittanica* (Chicago: Encyclopedia Brittanica, Inc., 1987).

descendant of the early Netherlandish school we covered in "The Charnys and Passion Art."

Roger Bacon (c. 1220-1292), Franciscan friar from England and born ten miles from Glastonbury Abbey, who in his 1267 work, *Perspectiva*, revealed a knowledge of light and apertures. In this regard Bacon is building on the work of Hassan ibn Hassan (died c. 1040, Egypt), who discussed the laws of reflection and showed an understanding of refraction in his work *Kitāb al-manāẓir* (*Optics*).[15] The Polish friar and scientist, Vitello (c. 1230-c. 1300), who studied at the University of Padua, wrote of "reproducing luminous images."[16] For Vitello, light was not only essential but from God by way of Divine Light.

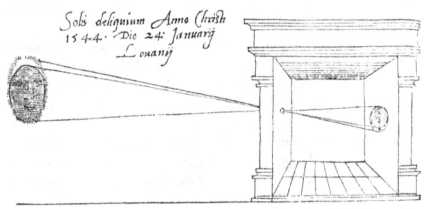

Example of camera obscura theory in Gemma Frisius' 1545 book *De Radio Astronomica et Geometrica*

Professor Allen argued, "[I]f a piece of linen, permeated with a dilute solution of silver nitrate is positioned inside a camera obscura, it can record (in the negative) the details of a sun-illuminated subject situated outside of the camera."[17] While light, of course, is integral to whatever means the image on the Shroud was produced, Allen's photographic hypothesis contradicts the sindonologist belief that the image appeared by an intense burst of light "so intense it could only have been supernatural."[18] Allen counters the claim the Shroud is a perfect negative photograph: "[T]he image is unlike a modern photographic negative in that it is not a snapshot of a particular moment in time, but rather the record of the original

---

15 Azzedine Boudrioua, et al., *Light-Based Science: Technology and Sustainable Development – The legacy of Ibn al-Haytham* (Boca Raton: CRC Press, 2018).

16 Mgr-Gen J. Waterhouse "Notes on the Early History of the Camera Obscura" in *The Photographic Journal*, Vol. XXV (31 May 1901), 270-290.

17 Nicholas PL Allen, "A reappraisal of late thirteenth century responses to the Shroud of Lirey-Chambery-Turin: encolpia of the Eucharist, vera ikon or supreme relic?"

18 Michael Day, "Scientists say Turin Shroud is supernatural," *Independent*, 20 December 2011.

subject according to the physical distance of a particular feature of the subject from the prepared linen cloth."[19]

Other points of contention involve pollen grains purported to be found on the Shroud and the claim that the blood on the linen is AB positive. Regarding pollen, it is vital for one to review the history of pollen analysis on the Shroud, beginning with samples taken from the cloth in 1973.[20] The findings of these, however, have failed to generate support outside the community of pro-authenticity Shroud supporters. The most vocal critic of the professed bloodstains on the Shroud was a former member of STURP, Walter McCrone (d. 2002), a renowned microscopist from Chicago. After a two year investigation of microscopic materials from the Shroud, McCrone parted with the findings of STURP and concluded the image and bloodstains were painted.[21]

It should be noted, from its first appearance and subsequent commentary about it from the anti-pope Clement VII (Robert of Geneva), the Shroud was not officially championed as the true cloth of Christ. That came later, during its long ownership by the Savoy, which maximized the relic to its fullest potential, particularly when Pope Julius II decreed the Feast of the Holy Shroud on May 4, replete with Mass and Office. In our own time, mainly through the homilies and reflections of the Roman pontiffs, the Church encouraged looking at the Shroud as a way of meditation and contemplation of Christ's sufferings while avoiding absolute claims of its authenticity.[22]

---

19 Allen, "A reappraisal."

20 See William Meacham, *The Rape of the Turin Shroud: How Christianity's most precious relic was wrongly condemned, and violated.* (Lulu.com, 2005).

21 See Walter McCrone, *Judgment Day for the Shroud of Turin,* 2nd ed. (Amherst: Prometheus Books, 1999).

22 See Anne Walters Robinsons, "The Man with the Pale Face, the Shroud, and De Fay's Missa Se la face ay pale" in *The Journal of Musicology,* Vol. 27, No. 4 (Fall 2010), 377-434.

CHAPTER SIXTEEN

BLOCKPRINT

U ntil the actual Shroud of Turin can be examined again, we are left only with speculations on the all-important image formation. But there is one other notion put forward by a former STURP member, Joseph S. Accetta, who has a Ph.D in electrical engineering (optics) from the University of Mexico, that must be addressed with its own chapter: the use of printmaking and blockprinting, also known as woodcutting. First, as an overview, one cannot separate the Passion of Christ with the makeup of the Shroud. It is a visual testament of the Crucifixion, a visual Gospel. Most notably, the blotch indicative of the centurion's lance wound (cf. Jn. 19:34). The blood marks around the forehead indicative of the Crown of Thorns (cf. Jn. 19:2, Mt. 27:29, Mk. 15:17, Jn. 19:5). The splashing blood wound at the wrist/hand and evidence of whippings. All of this plus seemingly unexplainable phenomena unique to the Shroud: three-dimensional imaging; lack of brush strokes or pigments; negative image; a superficial image only on the surface of the linen.

Joe Accetta suggests what we know as the Shroud of Turin today is "*remnants* of a 14th century blockprint (woodcut etc.) printed with iron gall ink.[1] Accetta notes Flanders and the general Champagne region was

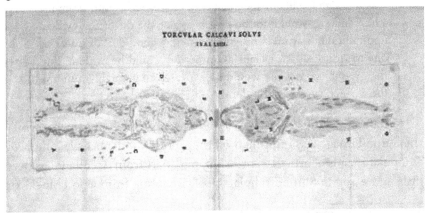

TORCVLAR CALCAVI SOLVS

Agostino Carracci (1557–1602) created this fold-out chiaroscuro woodcut printed in yellow ochre. The letters correspond to a key believers could follow meditating on Christ's wounds

1   Joseph S. Accetta, "Speculations on the 14th Century Origins of the Turin Shroud," presented at St. Louis Conference on the Shroud of Turin, 8 October 2014.

a major textile trading center, with the annual trade fair a major source of revenue and exchange of textiles. Accetta argues that the image we see today was not exactly what medieval viewers saw, particularly in its ostensions both in Lirey, Doubs, and later under Savoy ownership. This argument is complemented by the artworks depicting the Shroud, such as the Paleotti copy of 1598.[2] Accetta makes this point about dyeing linen:

> Due to the structural binding of the cellulose fibers in linen, the pigments will only adhere to the surface of the fibers. While linen will dye just as vibrant and deeply as other fibers, it will not retain its color as long. Exposure to air, light and chemicals speed the deterioration process.[3]

Accetta further notes that the relief printing process "transfers coloring matter in proportional to its local curvature and pressure,"[4] which would help explain the image's three-dimensional quality. This is a major point on which Shroud authenticity hinges: how can the image have 3-D properties? Accetta breaks down further:

> Image transfer from an object onto some recording medium can only occur by 3 processes; emitted radiation from the object, reflected radiation by the object and direct contact. Since there does not appear to be a radiative process vis-a-vis a lens, human eye or pinhole camera or other device with spatially invariant response that would give rise to the observed 3-d effect, we must specifically look to a direct contact process that renders an image density at least modestly proportional to the object feature depth. For several reasons, high fidelity image transfer in the case of a cloth wrapping a human body would not be possible since the distortion evident upon unfolding would be significant and a good deal of smearing due to front-to-back weight asymmetries would be evident. Further, the image density would be expected to be highly non-uniform which would not render the observed a 3-d effect.[5]

Accetta concludes woodprinting is the most likely means for which the Shroud image was imprinted on the cloth. Woodcuts have long been a popular means of artistic expression, but apart from Accetta it has been little addressed in Shroud scholarship. "[P]rinting from wood blocks on

---

2   See Andrew R. Casper, *An Artful Relic: The Shroud of Turin in Baroque Italy* (University Park: Penn State University Press, 2021).
3   Ibid.
4   Ibid.
5   Accetta, "Origins of a 14th Century Turin Shroud," 5.

textiles was known from the 14th century, but it had little development until paper began to be manufactured in France and Germany at the end of the 14th century."[6] Woodprinting was the common means for large-scale tapestries, with several woodblocks used to form the whole image. It follows, according to Accetta, multiple woodblocks were employed in the creation of the Shroud image, corresponding with the seemingly detached head image from the rest of the body. With this contact process, a number of hitherto unexplained phenomena become clear: 3-D effect, reversed contrast, details on the frontal and dorsal image.[7] Finally, the hematite found in the "blood stains" of the Shroud, with its high iron content, suggests iron gall ink.[8]

A contemporary artist from Italy, Davide Schileo, is a printmaker invested in the medieval and Renaissance production process of intaglio printmaking. His method is perhaps not too dissimilar to how the artist of the Shroud produced the cloth:

Artist Davide Schileo demonstrates his work | Courtesy Davide Schileo

6 "Speculations on the 14th Century Origins of the Turin Shroud."
7 "Origins of a 14th Century Shroud," 11.
8 Ibid.

EPILOGUE

Lamentation Fresco, Saint George Church in Asprovalta, Thessaloniki, 1550

CHAPTER SEVENTEEN

THE DIVINE LIGHT

The Shroud has donned numerous identities throughout its winding history. As we have seen it was first referred to in the Lirey
documents as a "figura seu repraesentatio" of the true shroud of
Christ. Under Savoy ownership, at least at the outset, it was referred by
Amadeus IX writing to Pope Paul II as "one of the shrouds of our Lord
Jesus Christ."[1] Later historians, such as Jean-Jacques Chifflet (d. 1660),
identified the Shroud as the means by which Joseph of Arimathea and
Nicodemus transferred the crucified body from the time of the deposition of the cross to the entombment. The idea that the image on the
Shroud was caused by an event none other than the Resurrection via an
intense burst of light which emitted from the transphysical body is currently popular among sindonologists,[2] though the Resurrection as cause
for image formation was first lobbied centuries earlier by Agaffino Solaro,
and a radical one at that, since the long-held belief was by bodily contact.[3]

While these sophisticated scientific notions are suggested as fact in
Shroud presentations, podcasts, and pro-authenticity books, they remain
only hypotheses. Widely overlooked is the theological controversy that
exploded in the Orthodox world that paralleled the presence of the Charnys in Achaea. It is known as the hesychast controversy.[4]

It is beyond the scope of this work to explore the theological, social
and political facets of this movement. But we would do well with a definition, from Antonio Carile, Italian medievalist and Byzantine scholar:

> Hesychasm is first of all the methods of monastic prayer and con-
> templation from hesychia, the technical term for a practice aiming
> to achieve communion with God through interior quietude, having
> at its core the "prayer of the heart," that is, the Jesus Prayer: "Lord
> Jesus Christ, son of God, have mercy on me," a prayer introduced

---

1 *Inter alia unum ex sudariis Domini nostri Ihesu Christi et quamplures alie venerabiles reliquie sint honorifice et decenter reposita; see Savio, Ricerche storiche,* 249.
2 For a summary, see Robert J. Spitzer, SJ, "Science and the Shroud of Turin," 2015 at https://magis-center.com/science-and-the-shroud-of-turin/.
3 Nicolotti, 220n78.
4 An introduction to the concept of divine light and the Shroud was presented at the 2019 Shroud Conference in Ancaster Canada by Mark Oxley, "The Divine Light and the Shroud of Turin."

to Mount Athos by Gregory Sinaites, who combined this continuous and imageless form of prayer with control of breathing.[5]

For the Hesychasts, this was not simply a quick-fix process of verbal repetition that would result in instant transcendence, but an experience that demanded total concentration in body, mind, and soul. "May your remembrance of Jesus become one with your breathing, and you will then know the usefulness of *hesychia*,' inner peace."[6] As Carile noted, Gregory of Sinai was instrumental in establishing Mount Athos as a bastion for the practice of hesychasm. Among his students was Serbian king Stefan Uroš IV Dušan, the seven-foot grandson of Stefan Uroš II Milutin.[7] This "Slavic presence on Mount Athos had a decisive influence in the Balkans."[8]

Simon Peter Monastery on Mount Athos | Gabriel from Bucharest, Romania, CC BY 2.0 <https://creativecommons.org/licenses/by/2.0>, via Wikimedia Commons

At the heart of the controversy were two monks, though the many tangled roots of the issue make it more than a simple theological argument. In any case, Gregory Palamas (d. 1359) was the key proponent of hesychasm and a monk on Mount Athos. A Calabrian monk known as Barlaam

---

5 Antonio Carile, "The Hesychasm in the Occident during the 14th Century," in *Thessaloniki as a Center of Orthodox Theology – Prospects in Today's Europe* (Thessaloniki, 2000), 131.

6 Benedict XVI quoting St. John Climacus in "General Audience – John Climacus," February 11, 2009.

7 Paul Pavlovich, *The Serbians: The Story of a People* (Toronto: Serbian Heritage Press, 1983), 35.

8 Carile, 132.

(d. 1348) took issue with the main belief of the Hesychasts, the nature of uncreated light. Also known as Tabor Light, to Palamas it referred to the light experienced by Peter, James and John at the Transfiguration on Mount Tabor, when the face of Jesus "shone like the sun and his clothes became white as light."[9] But this was not just a bright light. For the Hesychasts, it was the uncreated light of God. Moreover, this was not limited to those three apostles alone. It meant that when man experienced uncreated light, divine light, he was experiencing the divine uncreated grace of God, "the Energies shining forth eternally from the Divine Essence."[10]

Western Catholicism's Luminous Mysteries of the rosary, the Mysteries of Light, particularly reference the Tabor Light in the fourth mystery, the Transfiguration. Belgian author Ludo Noens attempted to equate this phenomenon of divine light with the Shroud of Turin, suggesting the cloth was created by a deeply spiritual monk on Mount Athos who became so immersed in the hesychasm prayer process and physical unity with the crucified Christ.[11]

In any event, Barlaam saw in this theology both heresy and blasphemy. "He also denied the reality of divine energies and claimed anything that was outside the essence had a beginning and was created in time."[12] But the Hesychasts believed what could be achieved was truly the same uncreated light viewed by the apostles at the Transfiguration, and experienced by other saints throughout time. Among them is St. Paul himself:

> I know someone in Christ who, fourteen years ago (whether in the body or out of the body I do not know, God knows), was caught up to the third heaven. And I know that this person (whether in the body or out of the body I do not know, God knows) was caught up into Paradise and heard ineffable things, which no one may utter."[13]

Ultimately, a series of synods in Constantinople presided by Andronicus III sought to resolve the controversy. Eventually, Palamas and the Hesychasts triumphed; hesychasm became Orthodox doctrine. Gregory Palamas was canonized by the Orthodox Church in 1368. Balaam, after returning to Calabria, converted to Roman Catholicism. But it is important to note that a broader movement was underway at the same

---

9   Mt 17:2

10 Vladimir Lossky, *Mystical Theology* (Yonkers: St. Vladimir's Seminary Press, 1976), 88-89.

11 Ludo Noens, Sublime *Light on the Turin Shroud: The True Origin of a Controversial Medieval Relic* (Brussels: Standaard Uitgeverij, 2015), 195.

12 Anita Strezova, *Hesychasm and Art: The Appearance of New Iconographic Trends in Byzantine and Slavic Lands in the 14th and 15th Centuries* (Canberra: ANU Press, 2014), 43.

13 2 Corinthians 12:1-4

time. Though the Byzantine empire was restored after the ousting of the Latin empire in 1261, western influence continued to spread into the next century. The empire never achieved the heights of its former glory. A civil war erupted from 1341-1347. It also was not immune to the Black Death. The quest for Byzantine identity thus fell into two camps: those who promoted venerable Byzantine monasticism, such as Mount Athos with its semi-autonomy, and those who supported a new humanism inspired by the ancient Greek philosophers as well as the leading humanists in Italy, such as Petrarch and Boccacio.[14] This would also describe Barlaam of Calabria.[15] There was also increasing reliance from the Byzantine emperors on the pope and the west, with frequent intermarrying into Latin nobility, such as Andronicus III's marriage to Anna of Savoy.

But let us return to the uncreated light. Through the practice of hesychasm, exercise of purity, and devotion to the love of God, the committed monk gradually reached *theosis*, deification – union with God. Anita Strezova noted, "Hesychasts believed that Christians can acquire deification only by participating in the corporeality of Christ, in the Eucharist, where the bread and wine become the circumscribed body and blood of Christ."[16] This notion is also reflected elsewhere, in the west, in the writings of the German Dominican mystic Meister Eckhart (1260-1328). Eckhart spent significant years in the Alsace region, particularly in Strasbourg, about two decades after Jean de Joinville accompanied Blanche to Haguenau for her marriage to Rudolf of Austria. However, Eckhart was in the place at the very time Holy Grave monuments took hold in the Rhine basin. Though lacking the dynamism of later Entombments, as we have seen, these sepulchers poignantly invited the faithful to gaze upon "him whom they have pierced."[17] Eckhart's observation about the Eucharist reflects the hesychast belief about achieving deification through the Eucharist: "When, in the Last Supper, the soul tastes the food and the little spark of the soul captures the divine light, it no longer needs any other food, it does not seek outside and stands completely in the divine light."[18]

In the Holy Grave monuments with the side wound serving as the receptacle for the consecrated host on Holy Thursday, and where the gisant of Christ becomes a de facto altar of repose, that divine light the Eucharist promises is perfectly visualized. Here we return to the idea of kenosis;

14 Carile, 132.
15 Strezova, 9.
16 *Strezova*, 131.
17 Cf. Jn 19:37.
18 Isabelle Raviolo, "L'étincelle de l'âme et la cavité à l'endroit du cœur du Christ dans les Saints sépulcres monumentaux," in *Revue des sciences religieuses*, 88/1 | 2014, 65-94. See n32.

Christ, dead at last, is placed in a cave, just as he was born in a cave. Here in death, the effects of his Passion brutally evident, one sees how he emptied his whole self – kenosis. Yet this is only one part of the Anastasis, one pointing to ultimate victory over death. "The feast of the Anastasis in the Orthodox Church commonly celebrates the tripartite theme representing Christ's descent into Hades: his victory over Satan, death and darkness; his deliverance of the righteous from Hades; and his victorious resurrection on Easter morning."[19]

Recall the moment of liturgical dramas wherein the Three Marys, or Peter and John, emerge from the sepulcher hoisting up the abandoned linen cloths. Enrico Morini and Flavia Manservigi observed, "Only representing two different clothes (the 'bandages' and the 'hat' [head cloth]) it was possible to convey the idea of the Resurrection: the representation of a unique sheet maintaining the shape of a human body would not have allowed communicating the idea that the corpse had actually disappeared."[20] Christ's descent into hell, which we have already seen was central in both Robert de Boron and *The Gospel of Nicodemus*, is commemorated in the Orthodox Church on Holy Saturday. This is "the day that expresses the unparalleled experience of our age, anticipating the fact that God is simply absent, that the grave hides him, that he no longer awakes, no longer speaks, so that one no longer needs him to deny him but can simply overlook him."[21]

* * *

The Harrowing of Hell constituted a sequence in the fourteenth century German vernacular drama, *The Passion of St. Gall*, "which is considered the most complete and typical of early German plays."[22] Text from Psalm 24 was included here as a kind of announcement to the gathered something wonderful was about to occur: "Lift up your heads, O gates; be lifted, you ancient portals, that the king of glory may enter. Who is this king of glory? The Lord of hosts, he is the king of glory. Such is the generation that seeks him, that seeks the face of the God of Jacob."[23]

On this day, a body lay in the tomb. The human body of the God-Man, killed, his mangled and bloodied body in repose. Look, there is the burial cloth to prove it … look upon him, it says, whom they have pierced.

19 Strezova, 132.
20 Morini and Manservigi, "The matter of the position of Jesus' burial cloths in a poetic text of the Orthodox Liturgy and in Iconography witnesses" (EDP Sciences, 2015), 9.
21 Joseph Ratzinger, *Introduction to Christianity* (San Francisco: Ignatius Press, 2004), 294.
22 Sandro Sticca, *The Latin Passion Play: Its Origins and Developments* (Albany: SUNY Press, 1970), 157.
23 Ps 24:9-10, 6

Here, the function of the Shroud perhaps becomes clear: Christ already crucified, not yet risen; a sign of contradiction, but a duality paralleling the completely human and completely divine nature of the Son. A duality seen on the Shroud with the frontal and dorsal body image, and in the Anastasis icon where Christ pulls both Adam and Eve out of Hades. In the wholly unique dual image of the Son of God on the Shroud, we see a kind of diptych that can be opened and closed – like a door, like the holy doors of an iconostasis where we can peer into the Holy of Holies, its own veil separated by the death of Christ.[24] Or like the doors of death, the gates of hell, flung open by the crucified, imprinting his image in "the abyss of abandonment."[25]

The Anastasis – Christ triumphs in death, surrounded by stars framed by the mandorla, taking Adam and Eve with him

In *Portrait of a Young Man* by Petrus Christus (c. 1464), a figure resembling a young Philip the Good, father-in-law of Pierre de Bauffremont, count of Charny, absently holds his book of hours while gazing past the frame. On the wall behind the man is a plaque of the Holy Face, with text from the hymn of the Avignon pope John XXII (d. 1334), *Salve Sancta Facies*, below the image:

---

24 Cf. Mt 27:51
25 Ratzinger, 301.

"Hail, our joy,
in this hard life,
fragile, fleeting
and soon everlasting.

Oh happy figure,
lead us to the end,
that we may see
the face of Christ."[26]

But the young man gazes out, affixed by something. Truth moves beyond the frame, beyond even the tomb, beyond death, as the mourners discovered that first Easter morning. *"Non est hic,"* they are told. "He is not here…go, and announce he has risen…"

Portrait of a Young Man, face of Christ on wall image | Petrus Christus c. 1464

26 "Salve Sancta Facies" in Pedica, *Il Volto Santo nei documenti della Chiesa*, op. Cit., 133-136.

APPENDIX A

DRAFT OF LETTER FROM PIERRE D'ARCIS TO POPE CLEMENT VII, C. AUGUST 1389-JANUARY 1390[1]

The truth about the cloth of Lirey, which for a long time previously was exhibited, had been exhibited, and now again was exhibited, concerning which I intend to write to our lord the Pope, in the manner written below and as briefly as I am able.

Behold, I kiss with devotion the blessed feet, with all the promptness that submission owes. Most Blessed Father, the greater cares, which above all concern danger for souls and which, on account of the power of some, it is impossible for the weak to provide for properly, must be brought to the Holy apostolic See, so that by its caring providence all matters may be settled advantageously, to the praise of God and the well-being of the subjects.

Therefore a dangerous and, by its example, destructive matter, which recently occurred in the diocese of Troyes, I have deemed fit to be brought to the ears of Your Holiness, so that, by the providence of Your same Holiness, who does not cease diligently to watch over the interests of your subjects and to keep them from harm, it might be resolved with a swift remedy to the praise of God, the honor of the Church, and the well-being of your subjects.

Since indeed, Most Blessed Father, a short while ago in the diocese of Troyes, the dean of a certain collegiate church, specifically in Lirey, deceitfully and wickedly, inflamed with the fire of avarice and cupidity, not from devotion but for gain, arranged to have in his church a certain cloth, cunningly portrayed, on which was portrayed in a subtle manner the double image of a single man, that is to say his front and back; [the dean] falsely asserted and pretended that this was the very shroud in which our Savior Jesus Christ was enrobed in the sepulchre, and on which shroud there had remained the impression of the whole likeness of the Savior himself with the wounds that he bore; much more than throughout the kingdom

---

1   Used with permission by Andrea Nicolotti.

of France, this matter has been so widely disseminated throughout the whole world, so that people have flowed from all parts of the world.

For the purpose of drawing in those very people, so that by cunning cleverness gold might be extorted from them, miracles were fabricated there by certain men induced to this by the reward, who pretended to be healed during an exhibition of the aforementioned shroud, which was believed by all to be the shroud of the Lord. In attending to this matter, Lord Henry de Poitiers, of good memory, at the time the bishop of Troyes, struck by the persuasiveness of many prudent men, since it was his duty in the exercise of his ordinary jurisdiction, took it upon himself to investigate promptly the truth of this matter: many theologians and other learned men assured him that this could not in fact be the shroud of the Lord, because it had the imprinted likeness of the Savior himself, since the Holy Gospel makes no mention of an impression of this sort, while, however, if it had been true, it is not likely that the holy evangelists would have kept silent or omitted it, nor that it would have remained secret or hidden up to this time.

And finally, first by cleverness and care, and then by the gathering of information pertaining to this, he at last discovered the deception, and how [the image on] that cloth had been artificially portrayed. It was even proved by the artist who had portrayed it that it was made by work of a man, not miraculously wrought or bestowed. Therefore, after consulting in timely counsel with many learned men, both theologians and those skilled in law, and determining that he ought not and could not dismiss the matter nor conceal it, as required by his office he chose to proceed against the aforementioned dean and his accomplices for the purpose of rooting out that error.

They, seeing their malice had been uncovered, hid and suppressed the noted cloth so that it could not be found by the Ordinary himself; and afterward they kept it concealed for 34 years or so, until this year.

Now, however, with premeditated fraud and a view to personal gain, the current dean of that church, as it is said, suggested to Lord Geoffroi de Charny, knight, temporal lord of the place, that he see to it that the cloth be relocated to the church, so that pilgrimage to the church would be renewed and the church would be enriched by the proceeds. This knight, at the suggestion of that dean, who was following in the footsteps of his predecessor, approached Lord Cardinal de Thury, Your Holiness' nuncio and legate in the regions of France. He remained in silence about the fact that at the time it was claimed that the cloth was the shroud of the Savior, and that it bore impressed upon it the likeness of the Savior, and that the Ordinary had assailed against this fact, seeking the extirpation of an error which it had given rise, and that for fear of the Ordinary the cloth had been hidden, and even transported outside the diocese, as it is said.

He disclosed to the aforementioned Lord Cardinal that the cloth was a representation or figure of the shroud, to which many were led in devotion, which cloth previously had been held in the stated church with great veneration and had been frequently visited with greatest devotion, but because of the kingdom's wars and for other reasons, and at the command of the Ordinary of the place, it had been located for a long time at a safe distance and preserved in safe custody.

[Geoffroi] requested that he be permitted to place in the church the representation or figure of the shroud, to which many were drawn by devotion and were desiring to view, so that it could there be displayed and shown to the people and venerated by the faithful. The Lord Cardinal, not assenting to the entire request, but likely for a particular purpose, and therefore in this he acted wisely, granted to the supplicant by apostolic authority that without permission from the Ordinary of the place or anyone else, he could place or locate the representation or figure of the Lord's shroud in the aforementioned church or in a suitable place elsewhere.

On the pretext of this letter, the aforementioned cloth was displayed and frequently shown to the people in the aforementioned church on solemn days and feast days, and otherwise, openly,. With the greatest solemnity, even greater than when the Body of our Lord Jesus Christ was shown there, namely with two priests garbed in albs with stoles and maniples, very reverently, with torches lit and in a high, elevated place built especially for this alone. Of course in public it was not claimed to be the true shroud of Christ, and in a certain contrived way of speaking recently invented in the church it is not called the shroud, but rather the sanctuary, which sounds the same in the ears of the people who are not at all discerning in such matters.

A multitude of people flows to the place as often as the cloth is exhibited or is expected to be exhibited, since they believe – but rather, in truth, are erring – that it is the true shroud; and a rumor is going around among the people that it was approved by the apostolic See through the letter of the aforementioned Lord Cardinal.

Furthermore, I, Most Blessed Father, seeing so great an inducement to sin renewed among the people and an error of this sort growing in its danger to and deception of souls, and considering that the dean of the church was not content with the bounds set by the Lord Cardinal's letter, which nevertheless had been obtained by suppressing the truth and suggesting falsehood, as was already said, and wishing as much as was in my powers to oppose the dangers to souls and to destroy and root out such a detestable error from the flock entrusted to me, having again made timely consultation about this matter with many learned men, I prohibited the dean, under penalty of excommunication *latae sententiae*, from exhibiting or showing the aforementioned cloth to the people until otherwise might be determined in this matter.

But he, disobedient, having recourse to an appeal, going against the prohibition, preserved in exhibiting it as before; even the knight himself supported and defended this sort of practice, holding that cloth in his own hands on a certain solemn day and exhibiting it publicly to the people with the solemnity that I already mentioned; thanks to a safeguard of the king, he had the cloth kept in his possession with the right of exhibition and he had me notified of that safeguard. And so, under the protection afforded by both his appeal and the safeguard, that error is defended, maintained, and grows strong in contempt of the Church and as a stumbling block to the people because of the aforementioned facts that obstruct me; rather more it is asserted and defended to the dishonor of my predecessor, who pursued this matter during his tenure, and to my dishonor, who desires to attend to this matter during his tenure, and to my dishonor, who desires to attend to this matter in a proper and prudent manner – oh what a grief!

Rather, supporting this, they cause it to be spread among the people that I pursue this matter out of envy or cupidity and avarice, and so that I might seize the cloth, just as at other times my predecessor has been so accused; some even say that I proceed in this matter too tepidly and that the fact that it is tolerated is a mockery. And even though with earnestness and humility I urged and requested that the already-mentioned knight cease and refrain from exhibitions of the cloth for a time, until Your Holiness was consulted and made a determination, he did not care to do so, but in fact, unbeknownst to me, he had it reported to Your Holiness that which he had reported to the aforementioned Lord Cardinal, and that I, refusing to comply with the letter of the Lord Cardinal himself, and disregarding the appeals, would not cease to move ahead with prohibitions and sentences of excommunication against those showing the cloth itself and against the people who frequented that place to venerate it.

But, with all due respect to him who reported this, in proceeding in the aforementioned manner against the ones exhibiting the cloth and those venerating it, in no way did I contravene the letter, although obtained through deception, of the aforementioned Lord Cardinal, in which he had not granted that the cloth could be shown to the people or even venerated, but only that it could be placed and located in the already-mentioned church or elsewhere in a suitable place. Because they were not content with the concession of the Lord Cardinal, therefore I proceeded against them by right of the Ordinary, not without much counsel, as was them by right of the Ordinary, not without much counsel, as was incumbent upon me because of my position, with a view to removing the stumbling block and rooting out this sort of error, believing that it would not be without great blame if, with closed eyes, I were to allow such things to pass by.

But, looking to my own security in this matter, always relying on the counsel of learned men, it was necessary that I have recourse to the secular branch, especially when I considered that the knight himself had begun to put the case in the hands of a secular power, as was mentioned, by having the cloth remain in his possession and by having the right to exhibit and to display it to the people because of the safeguard of the king, which seems rather absurd; I saw to it that that cloth be placed in the king's hands, always seeking that goal, that at least while I brought the account of the matter to Your Holiness' attention, in the meantime there might be a suspension of the aforementioned exhibition, which I obtained gently and without any difficulty when the whole council of the king's Parliament was fully informed concerning the superstitious invention of this shroud and its abuse, and concerning the aforementioned error and stumbling block.

And everybody knowing the merits of the case is amazed that I am impeded by the Church in this sort of prosecution, I, who ought to be helped vigorously, but rather ought to be punished severely if I were negligent or remiss in this matter. But nevertheless the aforementioned knight, forestalling me and, as is said, referencing the matters which were stated above, at last obtained from Your Holiness a letter, in which it is said in fact, having confirmed the letter of the aforementioned Lord Cardinal and from certain knowledge, that it is granted to the knight that, notwithstanding any prohibitions and appeals, it might be permitted that the cloth be exhibited and shown to the people, and venerated by the faithful, imposing on me perpetual silence, as is reported, since I was unable to have a copy of the letter. But inasmuch as a canon requires me not to allow anyone to be deceived by worthless fabrications or false documents on account of lucre, I am sure that the letter has been obtained through the

193

suggestion of falsehood and the suppression of the truth, because otherwise it would not have been obtained without having summoned or listened to me, especially since the presumption ought to have been in my favor, a business of this sort without cause or to disturb anyone in their prudent and otherwise well-ordered devotion.

I am firmly confident that Your Holiness will uphold with equanimity that I resist the aforementioned exhibition, with the aforementioned issues in mind, until I receive different instructions from Your Holiness, once you have been informed more fully in the truth of the matter.

Therefore, Most Blessed Father, may Your Holiness vouchsafe to direct the gaze of your consideration to the aforementioned and provide for these matters in such a way that this sort of error and stumbling block and detestable superstition be utterly rooted out both through action and restriction by the providence of Your Holiness, in such a way that that cloth neither as a shroud, nor a "sanctuary," nor as a representation or figure of the Lord's shroud, because the Lordly shroud was not made such, nor by any other contrived way or name be exhibited to the people or even venerated. But as a sign of reproaching superstition let it be condemned publicly after having revoked the aforementioned letter obtained through deceit, rather, declaring the letter void, [lest by chance the grudging persecutors of the Church and the invidious detractors that irreverently offend the governance of the Church eventually say that against the scandals and errors a stronger and more advantageous solution is found in the secular court than the ecclesiastical one].

For now I offer myself prepared in readiness to inform you adequately and without hesitation through public opinion and otherwise about everything I alleged above with a view to my justification and exoneration of conscience concerning this sort of deed, which is very close to my heart, and indeed I would have personally come before the presence of Your Holiness to set forth my complaint properly, if the strength of my body had allowed, certain that I am not able to express fully or sufficiently enough in writing the weight of the scandal, the reproach of the Church and ecclesiastical jurisdiction, and the danger to souls; nevertheless, I do what I am able, so that I may deserve to be excused chiefly before God, relinquishing what is left to the disposition of Your Holiness.

May the Almighty see fit to preserve you auspiciously and for a long time as one useful and necessary to the guidance of His Holy Church. Written [etc.].[2]

---

2 Nicolotti, *The Shroud of Turin*, 90-96. See Chevalier, *Étude critique*, doc. G.

Appendix B

"Shrouded Connections: Serbia, the Shroud, and the Holy Face of Laon"[1]

In the mid-13th century, so the story goes, a man obtained an image of the Holy Face. He did not keep it for himself. Rather, he sent it to a Cistercian monastery northeast of Paris. Eventually, it was moved out of the monastery to a church, the cathedral of Notre-Dame in Laon. Hence the name of this image – the Holy Face of Laon.

The man was Jacques Pantaleon, the future Pope Urban IV, who sent the icon to his sister, abbess of Montreuil-les-dames. It was July 1249. Below the image of the face of Christ is an inscription in late first millennium Slavonic, *Obraz Gospodin na Ubruzje*: "the image of the Lord on the cloth." In an accompanying letter, Pantaleon commented on the darkness of the image: "the color of Christ's face is the result of his tribulations during his Passion, and of his peregrinations in the sun." Additionally, he urged his sister to look upon it "like the holy Veronica, as its true image and likeness."

About a hundred years later, another man obtained an image of not only the face, but the full body of Christ. He did not keep it for himself. Rather, so the story goes, this man – knight Geoffroy de Charny – installed a large linen cloth in a church at Lirey, just south of Troyes. It was eventually moved to the cathedral of John the Baptist in Turin. Hence the name of this image – the Shroud of Turin.

A problem with the Shroud is the many origin stories that attempt to explain its provenance. Career soldier and diplomat that he was, Charny might have simply viewed the cloth as just another trophy or spoil of war, if he even viewed it at all: there's no indication of it in any of his writings, in his petitions to popes, in the Act of Foundation for the church he had built in Lirey, or when the bishop of Troyes consecrated the church in May 1356. Four months later, Charny was dead at the Battle of Poitiers in the Hundred Years' War. Although he wished to be buried at the cemetery

1 Originally published in *Catholic World Report*, 7 November 2021.

of his Lirey church, Our Lady of the Annunciation, his body never made it back home. Was the presence of the Shroud a kind of *drap mortuaire* commemorating the deceased Charny in the meditative light of the visage of the crucified, entombed Christ?

We begin with considering two comments about the Shroud made from his heirs – the statement of his son, Geoffroy II, cited in a 1390 papal bull that the Shroud was "freely given" (*liberaliter oblatam*); and from granddaughter Marguerite de Charny in a 1443 deposition: "[the Shroud] was obtained by the late Geoffroy de Charny, my grand-father" (*fut conquis par feu messire Geoffroy de Charny, mon grant pere*).

Taking those vague comments at face value, the present scenario hypothesizes Geoffroy de Charny "obtained" or "acquired" the Shroud as a gesture of conciliation or diplomatic gift from the Serbian royal court of the Nemanjić dynasty. This would have been while Charny was in southern Italy at the time of his participation in the Smyrniote Crusades of the mid-1340s, but before the building of his Lirey church in 1353. This hypothesis proposes he had the cloth, rolled up or folded in a chest, stored in the nearby Benedictine monastery of Saint-Pierre de Montier-la-Celle in Troyes, eight miles north of Lirey.

Only after Charny's death in 1356 was it moved to the Lirey church, amid the destruction caused by the English invasion of Champagne. This, then, created confusion over ownership: was it the property of the church canons, or was it owned by Charny's heirs? Such a debate lingered for the rest of the Shroud's time in France, ultimately forcing the eventual owners, the House of Savoy, to invent origin stories of the cloth that simply did not hitherto exist.

But why southern Italy? A fresco in the church of Santa Maria del Casale in Brindisi depicts the Charny coat of arms – escutcheon with three silver shields – along with insignia of other crusaders. Marcello Semeraro argued that this heraldic fresco was commissioned by Charny between 1344-1346, as Brindisi would have been the port from which the crusaders set sail for Smyrna. This was in the time of Angevin domination of the heel of Italy, when Robert II of Anjou was prince of Taranto, king of Albania, prince of Achaea, and titular Latin emperor of Constantinople. Indeed, Robert and his wife, Marie of Bourbon, acquired two Frankish baronies in the Morea from the niece of Geoffroy de Charny, the baroness Guillemette de Jonvelle, in 1359.

About sixty miles north of Brindisi is another port city, Bari, with its Church of San Nicola (now a pontifical basilica) and its relics of Saint

Nicholas, venerated by both eastern and western Christians. It was in Bari where Jacques Pantaleon obtained the Holy Face icon. As papal legate for Innocent IV to Germany, and later Patriarch of Jerusalem, Pantaleon was *papabile* material, versed in the art of diplomacy and negotiation, so much so that his election to the papacy was a unique one – he was not a cardinal.

Andre Grabar remarked in his 1931 study of the Laon icon, "The faultless Slavonic inscription could only have been written in one of the three Slavonic countries which used the Cyrillic alphabet at the time: Serbia, Bulgaria or Russia." Let us then look closer at Serbia. Noel Currer-Briggs connected the Holy Face of Laon to a badly preserved mandylion fresco in the Church of the Annunciation at the Gradac Monastery, built between 1277-1282 by the Serbian queen consort, Helena of Anjou. Helena was a major figure in Serbian lore, a saint in the Serbian Orthodox Church, and crucially, a woman with western blood.

Helena and her heirs of the Nemanjić dynasty were significant donors to San Nicola in Bari. The wife of King Stefan Uroš I from 1243 until his death in 1277, Helena was the daughter of John Angelos (son of the deposed Byzantine emperor Isaac II Angelos) and, according to Filip Van Tricht, Mathilda of the Frankish house of Courtenay, which produced several Latin emperors of Constantinople. Helena's two sons both became Serbian kings, and Helena governed land in her own right, namely the province of Zeta off the Adriatic Sea. Helena also had a deep devotion to Saint Nicholas; she died at Saint Nicholas Church, which she had built, in the Kotor municipality. Nicole Sabourin identified Kotor as a particularly vibrant location for the production of sacred art.

The Epitaphios icon also emerged in the Christian east at this exact time, known in its liturgical usage as *Epitáphios Thrēnos* ("Lamentation upon the Grave"), and integrated in the Great Friday liturgies. An image of Christ recumbent in death, painted or embroidered on a richly adorned cloth, commemorated individuals of stature, deceased or otherwise. The epitaphios of Helena's son, King Stefan Uroš II Milutin, for instance, contains another Slavonic inscription: "Remember, O God, the soul of your servant Milutin Uroš." With this remarkable work, one can see the influence either *of* – or influence *on* – the Shroud, an extremely important distinction of prepositions in this case.

Given, therefore, the vibrant interplay across the Adriatic Sea, and if the icon of the Holy Face was given to Jacques Pantaleon in Bari as a diplomatic gift or donation, could the same be said of the Shroud "freely given" to Geoffroy de Charny? The Shroud encapsulates the intense 14th-century medieval devotion to the Passion of Christ, and one inseparable from the zealous interest in the Holy Sepulchre. And if one could not journey to Jerusalem, Jerusalem would be brought to them: relics, art, entombment sculptures. And a major influence on the new focus from Christ Pantocrator to Christ Crucified? St. Francis of Assisi and the Franciscans.

The stigmata-bearing Francis has been known as the "Christ-Image of the Middle Ages," Joseph Ratzinger wrote in his doctoral dissertation. Queen Helena strongly supported the Franciscans, such as building a Franciscan church within the Gradac Monastery dedicated to St. Nicholas. An icon of Sts. Peter and Paul preserved in the Vatican Treasury is believed to have been commissioned by Helena as a gift to the first Franciscan pontiff, Nicholas IV (1288-1292). Moreover, murals at Gradac depicted the Man of Sorrows; only a year after Nicholas IV's death, the Man of Sorrows imagery appeared in the west for the first time – from a Franciscan prayer book.

Interestingly, before ascending to the papacy as Nicholas IV, Jerome Ascoli was provincial minister of Dalmatia in a time and place which certainly introduced him to the hybrid culture of east and west Christianity. It was also a region that fell under Helena of Anjou's rule.

Before Francis's spiritual conversion in the early 13th century, his hero was the crusading adventurer Walter III of Brienne, the first Brienne to rule as Count of Lecce as well as Prince of Taranto in southern Italy. Walter III's brother was John of Brienne, king of Jerusalem, emperor of Constantinople, and veteran of the Fifth Crusade, where St. Francis himself attempted to convert the sultan of Egypt. John stepped down as Latin emperor, and donned the habit of an anonymous Franciscan friar. He is buried in the Lower Basilica of Assisi. Another Brienne had a chapel nearby – Walter VI.

Walter VI, count of the Brienne homeland in Champagne, thirty miles northeast of Lirey, was a close associate of Geoffroy de Charny. Not only did Walter VI and Geoffroy de Charny perish on the same day (September 19) in the same battle (Poitiers) protecting the same king (John the Good), they were also members of France's Order of the Star (*Ordre de l'etoile*). Charny's mentor until the Smyrniote crusade was Raoul I of Brienne, Count of Eu – Walter VI's father-in-law. We hypothesize, then, that the Count of Brienne, Lecce, and claimant to the duchy of Athens, Walter VI, was aware of Geoffroy de Charny receiving from a Serbian envoy the Shroud as a gift, for diplomatic purposes, or simply as a pious gesture of goodwill, and having it sent it to Montier-la-Celle.

After all, Charny needed permission from the abbot of Montier-la-Celle to build his church. It was an ancient, prestigious monastery, where St. Robert of Molesme entered the Benedictine order and St. Bernard of Clairvaux took monastic professions. The idea of the abbey as a secure place to store or donate an object like the Shroud is not far-fetched. Consider that both Walter VI's father and the count of Joigny each had a key to the same secure chest retained in the abbey. Walter VI also donated to the abbey, according to his 1347 testament.

The deaths of these two men, Charny and Walter VI, allowed for the Shroud to be "discovered." In 1359, Montier-la-Celle was looted, ransacked, and burned by the English, forcing nobles' safety deposit boxes, reliquaries, and liturgical vessels to scatter. This is echoed six centuries later, during World War II, when the Shroud was secretly ushered out of Turin to a Benedictine abbey, Montevergine, outside Naples. Thus, it's feasible to consider the Shroud was evacuated out of Montier-la-Celle during the Hundred Years' War to the new church built by the man who acquired the Shroud in the first place.

We know in Fremont's chronicle that even as late as the 1690s the canons of the Lirey church commemorated Charny's death each September 19 with a ritual involving a funeral sheet displayed in the heart of the church affixed to a catafalque (raised bier). In this way, a *drap mortuaire*, not unlike the Epitaphios ritual in the Byzantine world, commemorated Geoffroy de Charny, deprived of burial in Lirey, but uniting it with another missing body – the resurrected body of Christ.

As for Jacques Pantaleon, it may be simply a coincidence that he was a native of Troyes, and that his chamberlain was one Pierre de Charny (d. 1274), archbishop of Sens, who had the same coat of arms as that of Geoffroy de Charny. It might be a mere coincidence that a prior of Montier-la-Celle was a man called Jean de Charny, the same name as that of Geoffroy de Charny's father. This was in the 1380s – the same decade controversy around the Shroud would explode just down the road from Montier-la-Celle in Lirey.

And it may also just be a coincidence Geoffroy de Charny was counselor to the king for the region of Picardy – the same region where in a Cistercian nunnery was an image of the Holy Face, a face with not a few similarities to the face on the cloth freely given to that most "true and perfect knight."

COMMENTARY: SCIENCE AND THE SHROUD

Joseph S. Accetta, PhD.

T he authenticity of the Shroud is a subject fraught with intense debate. I think in the contemporary context, authentic means it is the burial cloth of Christ. Scientific proof of this hypothesis appears to beyond reach at the moment. In any case scientific theories are supposed to embrace a number of testable hypotheses. The more tests the theory passes the greater the scientific acceptance. Getting specific for the moment, if the Shroud is authentic for example it should be 2000 years old or so thus the dating of the Shroud was a rather decisive test. Radiocarbon dating wasn't available to us in 1978 because the required sample size for radiocarbon dating was too large and it is a destructive test thus as a venerated object no one was going to cut a large swatch out of the Shroud. Since that time, new techniques have been developed that required only threads of material and that enabled the dating process to move forward. In 1988 a dating of certain threads extracted from the cloth took place at University of Arizona, Oxford in England and at Rochester.

The results were fairly consistent with each other and all indicated a date of medieval origin reasonably consistent with its documented history. There is an ongoing controversy about the date obtained and the possibility that the sample might have been contaminated with medieval cotton. This is not an indictment of the dating labs nor was it just a conjecture by Shroud believers. There appears to be some legitimate reasons to at least review the process and maybe execute a re-dating just to make sure. There is nothing extraordinary about the existence of controversy such as these in scientific investigations. Nevertheless, this is the first step to scientific legitimacy

In these times we look to science to both shape and affirm our beliefs partly because it has brought us so many wonderful (and sometimes terrible) things. This is in interesting contrast to days long gone past when we looked to scripture and theology for affirmation. But religion is about faith and science is about experimental demonstration and at this time in history there is a great abyss between them.

To my skeptical colleagues I would say that there is no list of "authorized" subjects for scientific investigation. The alternative would constitute a kind of scientific chauvinism similar to the religious prohibitions and persecutions encountered by Galileo for example. Questioning the productive value of such an enterprise lying outside of mainstream science is fair but that really boils down to a value judgment. Besides, much basic science proceeds without regard to long term "value".

Because of the religious connotations of the Shroud, some in the scientific community question the ethics of these investigations however as is well known the study of religious objects per se has value outside of religion. An object may be simultaneously legitimate subject material for in multiple systems of belief. Biblical archeology is no less scientific than conventional archeology because it deals with religious objects. Sometimes I wonder if these criticisms are nothing more than a thinly veiled anti-Christian sentiment or the expression of agnostic or atheistic views. On the other hand, to my devout friends, I would say do not look to the Shroud for sort of physical affirmation of your faith or expect science to confirm what you already believe (because, as you already suspect, we are a bunch of pagans anyway.). For science of the Shroud to go mainstream requires the attention of historians, art history specialists, archeologists, conservationists and the like and for the Shroud research community to tolerate and embrace discordant views. That is the way science is done. You have to work within the system if you are going to gain its respect. Unless you happen to be a Nobel laureate, speculating about non-existent physics is counterproductive and will engender contempt from the scientific community.

There are different standards of belief for individuals, courtrooms and science to name a few. Putting on my pointy scientist hat for a moment, we are supposed to be hard core skeptics relying on only repeatable scientific evidence to be judged in the courts of scientific inquiry and are not to let speculation nor our predisposed beliefs get in the way of our good judgment." I don't believe therefore it cannot be" is a bad as "I believe therefore it is" are dangerous predispositions.

There are many people who believe the Shroud is authentic but proof by use of scientific methods is a whole different thing. For that to happen, the Shroud would have to survive a full blown scientific "inquisition" in the open courtrooms of scientific inquiry. Scientific acceptance involves a slow, self correcting collaborative process by subject experts. As Carl Sagan said (and perhaps others) "extraordinary claims require extraordinary proof."

Firstly of course it has to be 20 centuries old. If it is then it very definitely has a history before the 14th century and interested historians will no doubt have a field day searching for it and many dissertations will be written. The discovery of some secret cache of ancient documents like the Dead Sea Scrolls authenticating its history back to the first century would probably satisfy historical and scriptural authenticity requirements however broad scientific authenticity may well be forever eluded. I cite the obvious. We don't know what Christ really looked like nor do we have an account of any of his physical features. Although the cloth fully describes the scriptural account of the crucifixion in graphic detail, proof that the cloth actually ensconced the body of Christ escapes definition? We might speculate that at some point the blood (if it is conclusive shown to be blood) will reveal its DNA fingerprint however the blood is too fragmented to reveal this information. We don't know Christ's DNA..If we did what would it look like anyway? Would it be proof of His humanity..... or not. These things have all been said before. Given a 2000 year old date, the really vexing issue is accounting for the image in terms of 1st century technology and that in my world would be nearly impossible. Even its religious or theological value might be variable depending on which religious group you are a member of i.e. if you're Catholic it is likely to be important. On the other hand if you are a Baptist you are likely to be an iconoclast, already have all the answers you need and couldn't care less

The Shroud has thus far eluded mainstream scientific scrutiny for several reasons; (After all its just a piece of medieval linen with an image on it. How interesting could it be?) It's value to mainstream science is limited and the second because of the extremely limited access is there is a paucity of subject material on which to do physical investigations. Given full access to contemporary techniques, the 1978 investigations would pale in significance. So Shroud "science" proceeds in a very unorthodox fashion. Mainstream science does not deal with non-mainstream issues very well. Science usually has paradigms and precursors to guide its path. There are few here.

So to cast the cloth into the domain of mainstream arts and science for the moment it is, at best, of modest archeological and historical interest, perhaps of considerable scriptural/theological interest (although there is no explicit mention of an image in scripture) of interest to the art historians and art technologists and image scientists. That it is a manifestation of as yet a totally unknown "physics of resurrection" is at best pure speculation and at worst an oxymoron. God does whatever he wants whenever he wants for whatever purpose he deems. He has no mandate to render explanations to our hopelessly inadequate intellectual frameworks. These are matters for theologians to deal with.

Lastly, I have of late taken the view that if the Shroud is a 14th century creation then it must be accounted for within the technological, historic and social circumstances of that era. This "if, then" proposition leads me to assert, for a number of compelling reasons, that the image is the remnant of a high quality 14th century woodprint. I have documented this assertion in an accompanying paper entitled" Probable Origins of a 14th Century Shroud Image.

Index